Li'l Abner

A Study in American Satire

D1225752

Studies in Popular Culture
M. Thomas Inge, General Editor

Li'l

Abner
A Study in American Satire

by Arthur Asa Berger

UNIVERSITY PRESS OF MISSISSIPPI
JACKSON

First published in 1969 by Twayne Publishers, Inc.
Copyright © 1994 by the University Press of Mississippi
All rights reserved
Manufactured in the United States of America

97 96 95 94   4 3 2 1

The paper in this book meets the guidelines for permanence and durability of
the Committee on Production Guidelines for Book Longevity of the Council on
Library Resources.

Library of Congress Cataloging-in-Publication Data

Berger, Arthur Asa, 1933–
    Li'l Abner : a study in American satire / Arthur Asa Berger.
        p.   cm. — (Studies in popular culture)
    Originally published: New York : Twayne, [1970].
    Includes bibliographical references (p.) and index.
    ISBN 0-87805-712-9 (cloth). — ISBN 0-87805-713-7 (pbk.)
    1. Capp, Al, 1909–1979   Li'l Abner.   2. Satire, American—History and
criticism.   I. Title.   II. Series: Studies in popular culture (Jackson, Miss.)
PN6728.L5B47   1994   94-17079
741.5'092–dc20   CIP

British Library Cataloging-in-Publication data available

For Phyllis, Miriam and Gabriel

Contents

Illustrations

Preface

They laughed when I sat down at the typewriter! My colleagues and friends found it quite comical to think of someone writing a book on Li'l Abner, and I must say that I received a good deal of ribbing and kidding about it. However, I had a good time writing it and recall many occasions when, after reading some of the strip, I could not constrain myself and laughed until the tears rolled down my cheeks. Too bad that all scholarship can't have such happy associations. I was fortunate to work on a subject I enjoyed and hope my book reflects the pleasure I had in writing it.

I was aided by the excellent advice of Mary Turpie, George Hage, Dimitri Tselos and, especially, Mulford Sibley, all of the University of Minnesota. They were kind enough to read the manuscript and offer many valuable suggestions.

Some of the research was done in Italy, and I am indebted to Agostino Lombardo, currently professor of literature at the University of Rome, who suggested I write an article for his brilliant review *Studi Americani* on Italian and American comics. This article was used as the first chapter of this book. I am also grateful to a number of Italian writers and scholars, such as Umberto Eco and Giuseppe Gadda

Conti, who gave me the benefit of their friendship and assistance. Also, Miss Cipriana Scelba, Director of the Commissione Americana, has been most kind and has sent me clippings and other material dealing with the comics over the past few years. The original draft of this book was presented as a Ph.D. thesis in American Studies at the University of Minnesota.

I owe special debts of gratitude to David Noble, a student of American culture with truly eclectic interests, who has encouraged me by word and example, and to Jacob Steinberg, President of Twayne, and his staff, for expert editorial assistance. My wife Phyllis Wolfson Berger has been a most diligent critic and enthusiastic supporter. Grateful acknowledgements are paid to Al Capp for permitting reproductions of his comic strip, "Li'l Abner," to be used as illustrations for this book.

San Francisco   A. A. B

Introduction

I

This study begins where other analyses of the comics[1] have generally ended: with a serious and detailed examination of style and the way it is related to meaning. To my knowledge it is the first sustained critical study of a single comic strip. I have chosen to write on Al Capp's "Li'l Abner"[2] because it is one of the few strips ever taken seriously by students of American culture and because I think the quality of Capp's imagination is worthy of serious examination.

Literary scholars have tended to snub comics—dismissing them as purely commercial ventures by commercial hacks—and the attention of social scientists has generally been confined to their contents, so it is possible to say that comic strips have been rather neglected. The fact that hundreds of millions of people read comics does not mean that they are automatically important—although I cannot help thinking that this is significant—but it does not mean that they are automatically unimportant.

After a short discussion of popular culture and some of the controversies that rage about it, I shall make a comparison between American and Italian comics that appeared at approximately the same time and had similar subject matter in an attempt to show that the comics are often accurate reflections of value configurations. This is Part I of the study. In Part II, I shall trace the satirical antecedents of "Li'l Abner" and show how it draws upon certain aspects of American humor that are generally considered "native," and, in particular, upon American Southwestern humor. Next, in Part III, I shall make a detailed analysis of the humor in "Li'l Abner," paying special attention to Capp's use of language and his narrative and graphic style. I shall also focus upon Capp's treatment of certain subjects (such as love, marriage, the family, politics, business, etc.) in an effort to see how Capp mirrors American values and the conflicts we feel about them.

In my conclusion, Part IV, I shall discuss such things as the relation between American values and what I have found in the strip, suggesting other areas for investigation of the comics and related fields.

II

I faced a number of methodological problems in making this study. Although I have tried to suggest and answer them at various points in the work, I feel that I should now comment upon them briefly. The most important of these questions are: (1) Why write about comic strips? (2) Why this comic strip? (3) On what basis should episodes from the strip be chosen? (4) What is the relationship between Al Capp's

14

subject matter and technique and American society? I shall answer the first question in the initial chapter, which deals with popular culture and the comics. In this chapter I shall argue that we cannot afford to overlook popular culture, because in doing so we may gain a distorted picture of American society. I shall also suggest that it is often hard to make a valid distinction between popular culture and "high" culture.

The second question involves an assumption on my part —that Capp is worth studying. I consider "Li'l Abner" to be a very interesting strip, because of Capp's imagination and artistry and because of the strip's very obvious social relevance. I shall try to develop both of these subjects in my examination of the subject-matter and style of the strip.[3]

As for the third question, all I can say is that I have been forced to be somewhat arbitrary. I have selected some of what I consider to be the best, the most characteristic, and the most significant episodes for analysis. I have relied to a great degree on published collections of the strip but have taken material from it which has not been collected. Since "Li'l Abner" has been appearing for more than thirty years, it has been impossible to deal with it in its entirety.[4] To give some idea of the scope of the strip, I have made a classification of Capp's major subjects and interests—which will be seen to be quite far-reaching.

I shall try to answer the fourth question in various places—in my analyses of the implications of the form of the strip and some of its subjects—but I shall deal with the relation between the strip and American values most specifically in the conclusion. There I shall suggest that "Li'l Abner" is not simple and not mindless, that it mirrors many of the tensions that exist in our thinking and reflects many of our ideological commitments and values.

15

III

As a brief example of what an analysis of "Li'l Abner" can reveal, I suggest we take a look at the ending of Capp's story involving Kigmies. In this episode, Abner inherited fifty million Kigmies from an Australian relative and brought them to the United States. The peculiar characteristic of these little animals, which are part homing-pigeon, part bloodhound, part fish, part balloon, and part football, is that they love to be kicked. And, what is even more fascinating, they don't like to kick back. As one Kigmy explained matters, "We is a nice, safe li'l minority to kick around—WE don't kick back."[5] The political implications here are obvious.

Eventually Flash Manglebugle, the world's greatest promoter, becomes involved with the Kigmies. He has made millions selling people things they don't need, and anticipate making billions on Kigmies, things people *do* need. He says: "Those kick-loving Kigmies will absorb all the punishment man USUALLY inflicts on his FELLOW MAN!! It's the end of TROUBLE—it's the end of WAR!!"[6]

Just the opposite happens, it turns out, so Manglebugle is forced to isolate the Kigmies. He does this by trapping them in a huge underground cellar. They had unwittingly disrupted the natural order of society—fighting and scrapping—and had to be taken away. The following panels conclude the episode:

In the selection from the episode I have discussed and reproduced, we find a number of things that are typical of Capp: the fantastic creation that, by virtue of some incredibly good quality, poses a threat to a society postulated as being based on fighting, selfishness, and similar evils; the somewhat disreputable businessman—here a supersalesman

Ending of Kigmy Episode

—who exists by duping and exploiting stupidity and gullibility; ridicule of Pappy, who takes a beating "nothing HOOMIN" could tolerate; the ironic reversal which involves having the Kigmies learn how nice it is to kick, rather than be kicked; and a moral. The imaginative brilliance of the conception—an animal that thrives on punishment, a masochist that will absorb everyone's ill will, that will lovingly be a scapegoat—is not dulled by the fact that the Kigmy has religious, social, and political implications.

But a proper analysis of this episode, and of Capp in general, depends upon a more adequately elaborated discussion of popular culture (and the comics in particular), and an understanding of the background of American humor out of which "Li'l Abner" has grown. All of this is necessary for a true appreciation of both the formal or stylistic elements of Capp's work and what might be called his "social relevance."

Perhaps I have bent over backwards to avoid making the errors that John Cawelti mentions in his discussion of popular culture:

> Two assumptions about the character of popular culture have been largely responsible for our failure to develop a coherent conceptual system agreed on by historians, humanists, and social scientists, for the analysis of popular culture. These are (1) that popular culture is not only qualitatively, but generically different from "serious" culture and that, therefore, (2) a work of popular culture should be treated as something other than a work of art; that it can be meaningfully analyzed as a collection of social themes, a hidden ("latent") work of political rhetoric, a concealed bit of psychoanalysis, or an unconscious religious ritual.[7]

In order to avoid using "Li'l Abner" as *nothing but* a docu-

ment, I have probably erred in emphasizing its artistic qualities and certain formal aspects in it that I found interesting.
This has been partly forced upon me because an understanding of a comic strip involves an excursion into the nature of
such things as caricature, the grotesque, satire, and humor,
in which formal as well as topical considerations are important.

CHAPTER 1

Popular Culture, the Comics, and Society

I

Why is popular culture so unpopular?[1] This question is really more complicated than it seems, for we have a paradox: culture that is called "popular" and yet is, at the same time, "unpopular." There is more to this than just a verbal tangle—for the question suggests also that we can distinguish between popular culture and other kinds of culture—taking for granted, of course, that we all know what culture is.[2] The answer to this paradox requires another question: *with whom* is popular culture unpopular?

If something is to be called popular it must, logically, please a good many people. "Popular" culture is obviously unpopular with a large number of literary critics, sociologists, psychiatrists, educators, and others who are members of the more educated and sophisticated elements of society. As David Manning White and Bernard Rosenberg point out in the preface to *Mass Culture*: "that there have been far more excoriators of mass culture than defenders became readily apparent to us as we sought representative selections for both points of view."[3] Why it is unpopular is another matter. I would say that much of the time it is because we fail to make a number of distinctions that should be made.

The errors that most people make in thinking about popular culture involve, first, confusing the different meanings of the term "popular," and second, talking about popular culture generically and not about particular examples of it. According to *The Random House Dictionary of the English Language* the following are among the meanings of the term "popular": ". . . regarded with favor, approval, or affection by people in general . . . suited to or intended for the general masses of people . . . adapted to the ordinary intelligence or taste." As the term "popular" is generally used, all these distinctions become blurred, and that is the point of the question asked at the beginning of this chapter. Many works of culture for the common people do not please large numbers of them. After all, a great deal of what is *meant* to be popular (i.e., pleasing) never really succeeds. This suggests that the term "popular culture" is inadequate since it fails to distinguish between the *audience* and the *effect* or reception of a given "production."

Well then, who likes popular culture? The answer is nobody. Nobody likes popular culture *per se,* but a large number of people like certain specific works of popular culture and dislike other works. I like "Li'l Abner" and dislike "Bonaventura," for example. I think *Rashomon* is a brilliant film and *Il Gattopardo* a poor one.

At this point one might object, "Is it not possible to talk about art forms, to make generalizations?" I would answer, "Of course, but they must be guarded ones—and there are certain dangers that, we might say, pop up. Once you start rating art forms where do you stop? Why stop at the distinction (I would call it a pseudo-distinction) between 'high' and 'low' culture? Why not make distinctions between 'kinds' of 'high' art; why not make a hierarchy of high arts: the epic, the novel, the novella, the short story, the long poem, the short poem, the epigram, and so on, *ad nauseum*. And then, is tragedy 'higher' than comedy? Is satire 'lower' than something else? Quite obviously all this leads us into a pit, but esthetics is a pit and it's a pity. The best way out, so to speak, is to move *down* the ladder of abstraction and focus attention on particular works, whether they be 'high' art or 'popular' culture."

But what is "popular culture"? To answer this we must discuss certain distinctions that have been made between "the two cultures." Another term for "popular culture" is "mass culture," which refers to that kind of culture, art, pseudo-art—or whatever you will—that can be mass produced and mass communicated, that has been made possible by technological inventions such as the printing press, radio, and television. "High" culture is considered that which has "uniqueness," "individuality," and "integrity."

However, just because something can be mass produced and mass communicated doesn't mean it necessarily is "popular" culture. Symphonies and operas are broadcast on radio and television, and the Bible is the largest selling book ever printed. Where does one draw the line? And mass produced and mass communicated material can bear the stamp of a particular personality just as well as "high" culture. Indeed, if one of the purposes of art is communication, what sin is it to communicate to a large number of people rather than a small number?

This brings us to a second point: popular culture is held to be that which is a commodity, an impersonal *product* created to please as many people as possible. It does not have that "public be damned" quality associated with great art—or, that is, often associated with great art. But is *intention* a good criterion for judging a work of art? Even if one does not accept the "intentional fallacy," the fact is that a good deal of great art was "written to please," so to speak, was hacked out, even if the hacks happened to have been geniuses. Shakespeare had a very commercial outlook and Mozart supposedly wrote so quickly that he hardly ever touched a note he had written.

The only distinction that *should* be made is between that art which is good and that art which is not good, and whether culture is private, public, esoteric, commercial, avant-garde, or vulgar is not really important. If there is much trash in popular culture, there is also much trash in high culture. There are countless numbers of second, third, and fourth rate poets, novelists, playwrights, and artists as well as comic-strip artists, television producers, and movie makers.

Another point generally made is that a mass produced commercial commodity aimed at pleasing the largest number of people *must* have the simplest appeals, *cannot* raise objectionable issues that might alienate someone, and so forth. This is not actually true, as Leo Rosten pointed out in "The Intellectual and the Mass Media: Some Rigorously Random Remarks."[4] Here he gives *examples* of material produced by the mass media which did step on toes, as he put it. He refutes a number of the apodictic indictments of popular culture.

I would suggest then that the distinctions that have been made between popular culture and high culture are generally so vague and blurred as to be almost useless. To put it rather facetiously, there is much low-grade "high" culture and much high-grade "low" culture, and the intelligent thing to do is not to reject art *forms* but particular works of high or low culture. If it is silly to criticize novels— and we do not argue about the novel but about particular novels—is not it also silly to criticize the comic strip or the film rather than particular comic strips or particular films?

The terms we use tend to confuse us and prevent clear thinking. Terms such as "low culture," "high culture," "mass culture," and "popular culture," are loaded with emotional baggage and make it hard for us to deal fairly with works being discussed. And there are certain questions that arise: must popular culture be "low"? Is "unpopular culture" the opposite of "popular culture," and is what is unpopular necessarily good?

A better term for what is generally meant by "popular culture" would be something like "common-man culture" or "ordinary culture." Terms such as these point attention to the *audience* of popular culture, avoid the confusions created by the term "popular" and the emotions generated by sneer-and-snarl words like "low," or "mass."

Common-man culture is attacked not only for the supposedly necessary faults it has as a form, but also for the *effects* it is supposed to have. The following points are made by critics like Dwight MacDonald and Bernard Rosenberg:

(1) it is bad art and drives out good art (Gresham's law applied to culture).

(2) it is a narcotic and promotes escapism, fantasy, etc.

(3) it wastes time and money.

(4) it is generally full of violence, sex, and crudities.

(5) it gives a distorted picture of reality.

None of these objections can bear critical examination, for almost anything that can be said about common-man culture can be said about uncommon-man culture. Great literature is still being written; painting, sculpture, and poetry are still flourishing, and "art" seems very far from drying up. A great deal of so-called "high" culture has just as much violence, sadism, and brutality as common-man culture, and the "world-picture" of a novelist is not necessarily any more truthful than that of a comic strip writer.

There is one other objection that is often brought against common-man culture: that there is little difference between any given work of this culture (any two songs or any two singers, for example) and that success is a matter of press-agentry. While I would not agree with this, it raises an interesting question: if we assume that press-agentry itself is a kind of popular art, why then is one press agent more successful than another?

We might also ask the critics of common-man culture: *Where is the "mass man" who is the drugged recipient of the mass-media?* I have been looking for a "mass man" for years, but like the abominable snowman, he seems impossibly evasive. The fact is, I think, the "mass man" is just a conceptualization, a bugaboo meant to scare people. "Watch out," we are told, "or you'll become a mass man!" The "mass man" reminds me of something John Dewey said when someone asked him about the danger of putting something in "public hands." He replied that he did not know any hands which were not private, which did not belong to someone. It might be added that the errors that have been made in judging what "mass man" wants are notorious, and attempts to control him (in democratic states) have been rather futile.

There is one more important problem that critics of common-man culture seldom talk about—and that is, what alternatives are available to it? Is everyone expected to burn, with "gem-like" flames all day long? Do they expect men who work in factories or even clerks and white collar workers who must endure the drudgery and routine of office work to have the energy, time, and money to lead "exemplary" cultural lives?

Behind most of the attacks on common-man culture is what I would call an "elitist resentment," so that attacks on common-man culture are really attacks on the common-man and his values by people who consider themselves to be superior. Since these "superior" people are now denied the privilege of ordering the people around politically, they maintain "the divine right" of trying to push them around culturally. As H. Stuart Hughes has pointed out, "contemporary democracy and contemporary mass culture are two sides of the same coin,"[5] and thus we must accept cultural democracy—the free choice of readily available culture—as the logical consequence of political democracy.

This common-man culture has been attacked as not "really" being democratic because, it is held, the ordinary man has little to say about the creation of mass culture and the controls of the means of transmitting it are in private hands.[6] But this misses the point. Of course someone *in particular* creates this material and the "consumer" has, directly, little to say other than whether or not he will "consume" it. What is important, however, is that this material is available to large numbers of individuals who have choices and whose choices do affect, in turn, the creation of this material.

There is some kind of curious contradiction here. Common-man culture is attacked as a "consumer" art—created to cater to the popular tastes—and yet the "consumer" is represented as a victim of sorts. He is a victim of art that is created specifically to please him. It seems to me that the "consumption" critics want to both *have* their cake and *eat* it—and the logical conclusion of their attacks, which would, I imagine, involve forcing upon the consumer art that is created especially *not* to please him, does not seem particularly desirable.

I might add that I see no reason why one should hang his head in shame at the mention of the magic term "consumption." There is nothing intrinsically wrong with consumption. What irks critics of common-man consumption is that people do not consume the "right things"—that is, what the critics like. When, in rare instances, this does happen, it is no longer "consumption" but "good taste."

The point I would like to make is that we should stop thumbing our noses at common-man culture and recognize that there is much that is good and much that is bad in it, that much of it is valid, and that it is useful for the cultural historian. Common-man culture, along with "high" culture (to use the familiar jargon) can contribute a great deal towards learning about and understanding the complexities of a nation's "character" since it takes a perspective into account that is possibly neglected by "high" culture.

What I. A. Richards said about best-sellers we can say about all the various forms of common-man culture: "Exemplifying as they do the most general levels of attitude development, [they] are worthy of very close study. No theory of criticism is satisfactory which is not able to explain their wide appeal."[7] It is *silly* that so many scholars have taken no notice of it because it is everywhere, have neglected it because so many people pay so much attention to it.

II

While there is a considerable amount of material on popular culture in general, the field has not received a great deal of attention. There are studies of the movies, radio, the popular book, and the comics,[8] but there are no studies in depth of which I am aware that deal with one radio program, one comic strip, one television program, or any one work of popular culture.

Most books on popular culture tend to be anthologies of articles, written transcripts of symposia, or some kind of literary pastiche. This very fact is significant, for it shows that we have had a hard time in finding a format in which to come to grips with popular culture, or perhaps that we have been unable to come to grips with it. Thus, Leo Lowenthal's *Literature, Popular Culture, and Society* is a collection of previously published writings on, as he put it, the "theme" of popular culture. The same is true of Robert Warshow's *Immediate Experience*. And *Mass Culture* by Bernard Rosenberg and David Manning White is an anthology. Gilbert Seldes' *Seven Lively Arts* is a systematic study, but it was written in 1924, and in surveying seven different forms of popular culture, it necessarily gave a somewhat superficial treatment of each.

All these rather fragmentary studies can, I submit, give us only fragmentary insights into the way popular culture reflects American character, for it is difficult to achieve a coherent picture out of incoherent materials. I think that the various insights we get are valuable, but that it is important to have some longer, more complete studies of particular works. It is necessary, I feel, to develop some of the hints and suggestions thrown out in the articles on comics, and that many comics just *mentioned* should be rigorously analyzed. There are two reasons for this: (1) Possibly by discussing only one or a few episodes in any comic strip we distort it; (2) The strip may have more in it than we can get from skimming it. We are seldom satisfied with an analysis of one chapter of a novel. Why then be content with an analysis of one, or a few, episodes in a comic strip?

To my knowledge there are no sustained treatments of any comic strips,[9] and the few books that are devoted to the comics are either collections of articles or cataloguing efforts. Thus *The Funnies: An American Idiom* is a collection of articles edited by David Manning White and Robert H. Abel, and while its range is broad, it does not include the type of critical analysis that I consider necessary to assess any comic strip. The other books devoted to the comics— Colton Waugh's *The Funnies*, Stephen Becker's *Comic Art in America*, and Martin Sheridan's *Comics and Their Creators* tend to be little more than annotated lists and are descriptive rather than analytical.

The question that arises now is what should an analysis of a comic strip do? I would suggest that at least the following points should be covered if a comic strip is to be intelligently and adequately discussed: (1) graphic, narrative, and verbal style; (2) changes that have occurred in the style during the existence of the strip; (3) main subjects treated; (4) historical influences upon the strip's style and content; (5) values championed, attacked, or revealed; (6) popularity and history of the strip. One further refinement involves studying the comics of foreign countries so as to have a basis for comparing native American comic strips with others. Such studies are useful ways of pointing out differences in national values and in stylistic conventions.

The following section, which compares American and

Italian comics, demonstrates that there are considerable
differences in style between American and Italian comics and
also reveals differences in approach towards the matter of
authority. I made the study of Italian comics because I had
the good fortune to spend a year in Italy (1964) and because,
to my delight, I discovered widespread interest in the comics
there. The considerable differences between American and
Italian comics suggest that comic strips do have something
of a national flavor and do reflect certain aspects of national
character. The contrasts of national values in the Italian and
the American strips support my belief that "Li'l Abner" may
be regarded as a mirror of American values. In "Li'l Abner,"
authority figures, for example, are treated in the American
way rather than in the Italian way.

III

In this study of American and Italian comics[10] I am
going to discuss the differences in their treatment of certain
common themes and subjects, and will relate these differences to conventions of the media for each of these countries
and to differing cultural "consenses." My method will be
essentially one of textual analysis though, of course, some
historical information will be used.

I have used the word "comics" purposely, because I
intend to concentrate my attention primarily on humorous
fumetti,[11] many of which have certain classical dimensions in
Italian culture. While the French term *bandes dessinées* is
probably more correct in that it covers all kinds of *fumetti*,
the term "comics" happens, in this particular case, to be
quite accurate and acceptable. Comics may be broadly defined as a series of drawings, usually involving dialogue, in
which the adventures of a group of generally well-delineated

characters provide amusement and surprise for the reader. There are two basic kinds of comics: *anecdotal* or *gag strips*, which have completed and resolved little stories each day, and *serial strips*, in which the story may last weeks or months. In all comics there are generally recurrent patterns of events which appear and reappear in a thousand different variations and which the readers come to anticipate. There are certain basic similarities as well as differences in the Italian and American comics which I am about to discuss. We will see that in both countries there are certain subjects—animals, soldiers, etc.—that keep turning up, but the *treatment* of these subjects is different.

For example, it is interesting to note the ways in which the military is treated in American and Italian comics. The differences are so striking, in fact, that on the basis of this subject alone one cannot help coming to certain conclusions about the two cultures in general.

The great Italian "anti-military" comic hero is a character named Marmittone, created in 1928 by Bruno Angoletta. Like many of the early Italian comics, this strip is very simply drawn with rather stiff, wooden figures, plain background, and dialogue in the form of rhymed verse (which appears in captions underneath the drawings). As in many comics, the dialogue is not really necessary; it only adds details, although the rhyme and the humor of the poetry are very amusing. This type of comic strip does not have dialogue as modern ones do, but resembles an illustrated poem.

Marmittone is an extremely enthusiastic and zealous soldier who, as a result of his continued bungling or bad luck, always ends up in prison. Most of his adventures involve accidentally discomfiting officers or their friends and being sent to prison. Marmittone is not rebellious at all; indeed, he is just the opposite . . . he *respects authority figures*, exhibits no desire to "cross" them, and if it were not for the fact that he is "jinxed" or perhaps even "doomed," he would be a model soldier. The only thing negative in the comic is that the hero, for whom we have affection and sympathy, ends up in prison—a dark, empty room into which a symbolic ray of light is always seen filtering. Thus, what criticism there is of the military is negative and rather weak. We feel that *something* must be wrong if Marmittone, a goodwilled hero, can end up in jail, but there is no direct attack made on the officers; they are only obliquely ridiculed, and always at the *expense* of the hero.

This is not so in American "anti-military" comics like Morton Walker's "Beetle Bailey." In this strip, which is currently one of the most popular American comics, the common soldier consistently engages in a battle of wits with his superiors and generally emerges victorious. The Sergeant and the Captain in "Beetle Bailey" are both, it must be added, relatively sympathetic antagonists whose cupidity and stupidity endear them to the reader. It is the enlisted men who have the upper hand most of the time because they have the brains and because *authority is not seen as valid.* The Sergeant is a good natured, boisterous glutton, and the officers are fools.

What is more, the ridicule is often presented pictorially. In one recent episode, for example, the Sergeant is seen coming through the chow line in the cafeteria. He has a tray loaded with steaks, potatoes, salad, and so forth. "Wait," he says to the Mess Sergeant, "I don't have any celery." Nor does he have any ice cream, but the Mess Sergeant tells him that there is no room on his tray and adds that there is "no coming through the line twice." The dilemma is solved by stuffing celery in the Sergeant's ears and an ice cream in his mouth. He thus "succeeds" but at the price of becoming a clown.

There is no such pictorial ridicule in "Marmittone," in

which relatively little attention is paid to expression. A contemporary Italian military strip dealing with the adventures of Gibernetta and Gedeone is somewhat closer to "Beetle Bailey," though it retains the humorous poetry captions of "Marmittone," and still has a reverential and respectful attitude towards authority. Rather than ending in prison as Marmittone always does, Gibernetta and Gedeone generally are awarded medals. The "fall guy" or the victim, this time, is the blundering, suffering Sergeant. The fact that the awarding of a medal is seen as a proper reward for our heroes shows that the officers, the real authority figures, are still revered as *legitimate*. The Sergeant, who is, after all, only instrumental in executing the wishes of the officers is also, we must remember, an enlisted man who has risen but who is still *not* a true authority figure.

Quite probably Cimpiani, who draws the strip, was influenced by Walker, for his hero Gibernetta at times looks strikingly like Beetle. He has the same round head, his hair sticks out wildly from under his cap, his legs are as thin as toothpicks (this applies to all Cimpiani's characters). The only real difference is that Gibernetta's eyes are visible, whereas Beetle's are always hidden under his cap.[12]

IV

Mickey Mouse, known as Topolino in Italy, is probably the most important comic strip figure in Italy. He is the hero of at least one weekly magazine, *Topolino*, and a monthly one, *Almanac of Topolino*. Both magazines contain Donald Duck and other Disney characters and have some adventures that are written specifically for the Italian public. Almost thirty percent of the readers are between sixteen and thirty-four years of age, which suggests that a good many of the fathers of children reading "Topolino" also read it. Since the weekly edition has a circulation of 260,000 copies, and *Almanacco* has a circulation of 140,000 copies per month, it is obvious that a large number of children and adults see the strip.[13]

The Disney characters have a supra-national appeal because they are simple animals and indulge in slapstick-filled cops-and-robbers chases and other such action-filled activities that are amusing to all children. Donald Duck, Mickey Mouse, and their friends have also inspired a host of imitators so that there is now a comical cartoon character for almost every animal that exists.

But why should a mouse be so popular with children? Possibly because the mouse is a small, defenseless, "household" creature that most children have seen, with whom they can empathize, and of whom they need not be afraid. Historically, Mickey Mouse is a descendant of the mouse Ignatz in one of the greatest American comics, "Krazy Kat," which flourished between 1911 and 1944 (until George Herriman, its creator, died). But "Krazy Kat" was much different from "Mickey Mouse." Ignatz Mouse was a decidedly *anti-social character,* constantly in rebellion aaginst society, whereas Mickey Mouse is decidedly well adjusted, internalizes the value of his society, is on the side of "law and order" and conformism. He is decidedly comforting to children since he shows that submitting oneself to the value of a given order ends in well-being, rewards, and acceptance.

V

If we return, for a moment, to the older "classics" in the Italian and American comic repertoires, we find another interesting pair of "anti-social" animals, the American mule,

Maud (1906), and the Italian goat, Barbacucco (1909).

Both animals are pitted against human beings—the goat butts people and the mule kicks them, but there is an important difference in the consequences, for while Maud always ends up "victorious," the goat's actions always come to nothing. For example, he will butt a tree in which a boy and a girl are sitting and the fruit will fall down, which they then eat. On the other hand, all attempts to "tame" Maud, the ornery mule, are useless and people who try to do so are most always discomfited, though they might have momentary and temporary successes.

Maud is a rebel who succeeds; Barbacucco is a rebel who does not; and perhaps, in some strange way, they mirror two different attitudes: American individualism and the Italian idea that the "given order of society" is too strong to be bucked, that things are "fated."[14] Whether the fates are smiling or not is beside the point, for if things are ultimately fated, individual initiative and efforts are of no great importance—"whatever will be will be," as a popular song puts it.

Probably the best example of this reliance "on the gods," which can be, at once, a source of great optimism and pessimism, is the famous Italian comic hero, Bonaventura, who started amusing children in 1917. Graphically, Bonaventura is typically "old school" Italian—the figures are stiff and crudely drawn, little attention is paid to landscape (which is highly stylized and greatly over-simplified), there is not much expression on the faces of the characters, there is much fantasy, and the dialogue is given in captions of rhymed verse.

Bonaventura is not a character for whom things *always* turn out well, though most often they do. When he instigates actions and activities—such as trying to drive a car, or trying to become a social lion—things turn out badly for him and he generally retreats and goes back to simpler ways and more secure activities. It is only when what seem to be chance "disasters" happen to him (and the malicious acts of his nemeses are also chance events) that happy consequences result and he earns his *milione* ("million").

Thus, at the end of an episode in which Bonaventura tries to drive automobiles, with calamitous results, he decides that in the future he will walk, or at the end of his adventure in which he tries to "enter society," he decides that society is full of delusions and that he will remain with his sweet and good family. For reasons such as these, I think we can call Bonaventura a decidedly *conservative* character, or one who embodies a conservative outlook towards experience.

This, in turn, suggests that "Bonaventura" is not really as optimistic a strip as is commonly believed, since, generally speaking, a conservative tends to be less optimistic than a radical. Bonaventura's "rebellions" against the more cloying aspects of family life or the limitations of being a pedestrian end in defeat. And even when he gets his *milione* it is generally the result of a freak occurrence in which he has been involved; it is always rather "miraculous." Individual initiative is played down, luck is all, and the best of all possible rewards is seen as money. Bonaventura is a materialist who symbolizes for his readers that the only way one can become a success in the world is as the result of a miracle . . . and this is not particularly hopeful.

Several other comparisons between American and Italian comics suggest themselves—attitudes toward royalty and aristocracies and the treatment of the "mischievous" child.

Otto Soglow's "Little King," which started appearing in 1934, is very close to the classical Italian comic in style, but far different in attitude. The "king," a fat dwarf who has a big mustache, always wears his crown, and generally wears an ermine robe, is humanized. He fetches the milk in the morning, he rushes to bargain clearances in department stores, and is generally shown to be "just like anyone else." He is made into a good democrat and there is no suggestion of any divinity "that doth hedge a king." Indeed, both the title of the strip, and the fact that the little King is mute, indicate this.

Antonio Rubino's "Lola and Lalla" is much different. Lola, the daughter of a rich man (we have here an aristocracy of wealth), is always elaborately dressed and quite vicious towards Lalla, her social inferior. Lalla is always shown in "modest but clean" clothing, decidedly inferior to that of Lola. As a result of being pushed around by Lola, however, she ends up with more beautiful clothing. Generally this is accomplished by having some sticky substance fall on Lalla, to which flower blossoms or something similar become attached.

The aristocracy, as represented by Lola, is seen as vicious and brutal, repulsing any attempt by the common people (Lalla) to be friendly, or to gain recognition. Social class is shown by clothing, as in "The Little King," but whereas the King is warm and very human, as we might expect from a democratic American king, the European aristocracy is demonic and insists that the people "know their place." Social mobility is impossible and any attempts at it are repulsed. Even Lola's dog, conventionally a friendly animal, is shown as nasty and cold, corrupted, we imagine, by his relationship with Lola and the "upper classes."

A relatively similar attitude exists in Italian comics dealing with "naughty" children. In many of the episodes the mischievous child is caught and punished; the price of rebellion is a spanking or some kind of humiliation. This is different from many American comics in which the child often succeeds in his pranks.

Take, for example, Rubino's remarkable strips "Pierino" and "Quadratino," which appeared in 1909. Pierino is a little boy who is always trying to get rid of his doll, but never succeeds in doing so. He buries it, he gives it away, he throws it down the chimney—but no matter, it keeps coming back. Generally in the last panel the same shaft of light that fell on Marmittone in jail, falls on Pierino, although in this case the ray of light probably symbolizes internalized conscience, rather than socially "objectionable" activities as in the case of Marmittone.

Quadratino is a boy whose head is a square. His escapades generally result in his head getting changed in shape, so that the fact that he has committed "crimes" becomes obvious, objectively visible. There is much distortion in the strip and a .good deal of plane geometry. But the moral of "Quadratino" (and of "Pierino") is that bad boys always get caught or, in more general terms, *rebellion against properly constituted authority is perilous and futile.*

It might be objected that Hans and Fritz, the "Katzenjammer Kids," also usually end up being punished, and this is true, but there is an important difference to be noted between the endings in the "Katzenjammer Kids" and in Rubino's strips. Generally, the pranks of Hans and Fritz are successful and cause a great deal of discomfort to the adults against whom they are directed. Thus, the pranks are successful as pranks. It is only that adults, having a monopoly on force, can get their revenge—and do so in a way that pales the victories of the kids (and tans their hides) .

VI

Let me summarize the underlying psychological and social attitudes we have found in these comics, and which I

41

am hypothesizing might be broadly accepted cultural values:

ITALIAN COMICS

CHARACTER	PERSONALITY TRAITS, ETC.
Marmittone	respects constituted authority, zealous, but jinxed
Gibernetta	respects authority
Barbacucco	unsuccessful in his rebellion against people
Bonaventura	bad luck usually turns out miraculously for the best, conservative approach to experience
Lola and Lalla	intercourse between classes impossible, upper classes seen as demonic
Quadratino Pierino	rebellion against authority (adult world) seen as futile

AMERICAN COMICS

CHARACTER	PERSONALITY TRAITS, ETC.
Beetle Bailey	authority not recognized as valid
Mickey Mouse	values of the given order are valid
Ignatz Mouse	anti-social and rebellious
Maud	anti-social and rebellious (successfully)
Little King	democratic 'king"—no different from anyone else
Katzenjammer Kids	rebellion against adult world successful in short run, but often has bad consequences

The conclusion that we reach from these particular cases is that the Italian comics reflect a basically conservative approach towards experience and society. Authority is generally seen as valid, and rebellion against it as futile. Social mobility is seen as essentially miraculous in a rigid and hierarchical society in which all attempts to climb are brusquely repulsed.

The American comics, on the other hand, suggest a basically "irreverential" approach towards authority. Authority is seen as invalid and not necessarily worthy of allegiance. Because of this, naturally, much more anti-social and rebellious activity is viewed as possibly successful. Except for the conformist, Mickey Mouse, all the American comics mentioned above are rebellious and tend to see authority as invalid. Mickey Mouse is, as I have pointed out, extremely popular in Italy.

These conclusions are, of course, tentative ones. They have been drawn from a limited reading of a small group of comics and quite possibly, because of this, are somewhat distorted. On the other hand, I have tried to discuss some of the most important comics, and to guard against unfair comparisons have also tried to analyze comics that were contemporaries.

It so happens that the attitudes about authority that I have discovered in the American comics square with the findings of some social scientists and with the insights of De Tocqueville and other travelers. Interestingly enough, my findings in the Italian comics are similar to the findings or opinions of a number of writers on Italian society. For example, the Bompiani *Literary Almanac for 1964* has a number of articles which suggest that today's Italian youth respects authority and is not particularly rebellious.

VII

As a postscript on the contemporary "comical" scene in Italy, I would say that currently the comic book industry is flourishing there, as it is almost everywhere else in the world, particularly since the end of World War II. Comics have a long history in Italy—but at the present moment, most of the comics published are either American comics which have been translated or imitations of American ones, generally in either the Disney "animal" school or the Caniff "realism" school.

Most of the "classic" old Italian comics are no longer being produced and, in a sense, it may be said that the *Corriere Dei Piccoli* has lost its "integrity." It now tends to follow the lead of television and to print *fumetti* full of sentimental slush and "innocent romance" (such as Dr. Kildare) based on television heroes. It seems to be floundering with no clearcut picture of its audience or what it should emphasize.

In 1961 a number of the publishers approved a "Moral Code" in order to prevent the government from "stepping in" with some kind of censorship. This code lists certain taboos which the publishers are to observe, including:

1. no discussion or doubts of the principles of family unity, marriage, *authority*, or of respect for parents.

2. no speaking of divorce.

3. nothing to cause lack of respect for Italy, the flag, democratic principles, or the institutions of the state.

4. nothing racist, or anything to offend human dignity.

5. no irreverent treatment of religion or casting doubt upon the utility of school.

6. as little violence, sex, bad language, or bloody horror scenes as possible.

This code is just an explicit statement of the conservatism found in the older Italian comics. Being humorous, they tended to avoid the pitfalls the code was designed to eliminate, though on the other hand, there was a great deal of violence in them. The code was apparently made on the basis of a contention that young children are not capable of intellectually or emotionally assimilating complexities dealing with the family, justice, religion, and so forth, and that it is best to present them with "security fostering" heroes, heroines, and stories.

While all this is possibly true in theory, and the code, no doubt, is the result of both a certain amount of good will and a great measure of shrewdness,[15] there can be no question that it is impossible to legislate "correctness" in the comics, and that many of the values espoused by acceptable heroes are possibly socially disfunctional.

Take "Popeye" ("Bracchio di Fero") for example. Rather curiously, the strip is now being run on the pages of the Communist daily newspaper, *L'Unita*. This is perfectly understandable; that is, if the cartoon editor (or whoever chose "Popeye") is a Leninist—for the strip's hero is an exponent of violence. In a typical episode he is one of a group of judges of a beauty contest. A number of beautiful girls parade past, but he does not like them. Finally Olive Oyl, his thin, ugly girl friend, comes by—number thirteen among the contestants—and he decides she should be given the prize. The other judges disagree; so Popeye knocks them out and awards the prize to his girl friend. "What's just is just," he says to Olive Oyl, "isn't that true?" "Of course," she answers.

On the other hand, we must realize that in this particular strip, and in many others, violence is a *convention* of sorts, a means to an end, but one which somehow is painless, has no bad effect, and therefore is seen as "funny." In the beauty contest story, there are several morals that may be drawn: that "love conquers all," that loyalty is commendable, that Popeye is a terrible judge of beauty, that there is "hope" for ugly girls, and so on. We must realize that *violence* in the comic strip is an extremely involved matter, and we must remember that there are numerous conventions which the readers learn that qualify it and almost everything else. (I have not mentioned the moral issues raised by this adventure: Is violence for a "good" cause justifiable? What is a "good" cause? These are questions that are, I believe, within the grasp of many of the readers of this strip and other comics, and upon which, in simpler terms, their unconscious and their consciences quite possibly might be stirring.)

VIII

In "Li'l Abner," there are numerous episodes which involve authority figures and which reflect a basic American approach towards them. We find a tension between grudging respect for authority, *ex officio*, and strong democratic egalitarian sentiment, a feeling of being equal, somehow. We find a good example of this in an adventure in which Abner's brother, Tiny, and his boss, J. Roaringham Fatback, have discovered strange little creatures called Abominable Snow-hams. Fatback wants to roast one, but Tiny won't let him unlesss convinced that they aren't human. Fatback fires Tiny and starts roasting a Snow-ham. Tiny says to himself, "Now that ah is FIRED—Ah don't hafta RESPECK him

46

no mo'! "[16] and prevents Fatback from continuing. Fatback was due respect because of his position but Tiny, ignorant as he is, did not consider himself to be inferior to Fatback and even went so far as to prevent him from doing something that was morally questionable. It is hard to imagine an Italian comic-strip character doing this type of thing.

In another episode in "Li'l Abner," a somewhat sub-human fiend named Dumpington Van Lump falls down the elevator shaft of one of his high-rise office buildings and commands his janitors to get him out:

VAN LUMP:	The only way to get me out of here is to tear this building down!!—as the owner of this building I order you to TEAR IT DOWN!!
FIRST JANITOR:	Gulp!!—If we tear it down WE'RE OUTA JOBS—an' you knows how hard it'll be for US t'get NEW ones!!
SECOND JANITOR:	Still, HE'S the boss. We've GOTTA tear it down!!
FIRST JANITOR:	SURE, we gotta—but he didn't say HOW FAST!! Hm-m . . . Doin' it ONE BRICK AT A TIME—will take us around 12 YEARS!!
SECOND JANITOR:	And THEN we'll be eligible for OLD-AGE PENSIONS!! We'll begin right after lunch!![17]

Here the authority figure is outsmarted, though respected, which implies that authority's validity is somehow question-able and that its scope is limited.

CHAPTER 2

Li'l Abner's Place in American Satire

I

Before I discuss "Li'l Abner" itself, I think I should say something about what satire has generally been construed to be. According to Northrop Frye, who has written extensively on the subject, satire has two essential ingredients:

> One is wit or humor founded on fantasy or a sense of the grotesque or absurd, the other is an object of attack. ... To attack anything, writer and audience must agree on its undesirability, which means that the content of a great deal of satire founded on national hatreds, snob-

bery, prejudice, and personal pique goes out of date
very quickly.[1]

This might explain why "Li'l Abner" does not appear in
Italy. I asked a number of Italian comic strip editors and
writers about this and the reason they usually gave was that
"Li'l Abner" is "too American" for the Italians. By this
they meant that it is based so much on national "hatreds"
and other things which Americans take for granted that
Italians cannot "get it."

Gilbert Highet has characterized satirical stories and
plays as tending to be episodic (if long) and improbable,
which gives the satirist a certain amount of freedom:

> Therefore gaps and interruptions, even inconsistencies,
> in the story scarcely concern him. His characters flit
> from one amusing humiliation to another with scarcely
> any intervals of time and reflection. Seldom do they de-
> velop by degrees, as people in real novels do.[2]

Highet makes another point that is particularly applicable
to "Li'l Abner": "Their heroes and heroines suffer more
trials and tribulations than any ordinary man could endure
without breaking down, going mad, or dying. They survive,
apparently untouched, apparently indestructible."[3]

It is this indestructibility that gives "Li'l Abner" a
touch of the legendary, for its characters often have somewhat superhuman attributes.

Despite these rather fantastic characters, satire is essentially intellectual; it assumes distinct moral norms and standards against which it measures the objects of its attacks. In
fact, Frye sees satirizing as a moral act:

> Satire demands at least a token fantasy, a content which
> the reader recognizes as grotesque, and at least an im-
> plicit moral standard, the latter being essential in a

militant attitude toward experience. . . . The satirist has
to select his absurdities, and the act of selection is a
moral act.[4]

What Frye suggests here is that a satirist must necessarily
make a commitment, either positively about what he wants
in a good society, or negatively, about what he does not want.
He then "pushes" his views through satire.

It should be kept in mind that just as satire involves
some kind of consensus and agreement between the audience and the satirist on what is desirable, caricature, which
is a type of pictorial satire, makes the same demands. We
find here what Werner Hoffman calls a paradox:

> While caricature breaks with the canon of beauty, dis-
> places the "normal" recognized pattern, and deforms
> the world of proportion, performing a subjective artistic
> act of release, it simultaneously binds itself indissolubly
> to the model it is dethroning. Caricature, like every rev-
> olutionary, is sustained by the system it attacks.[5]

This is a valuable insight, I believe, because it reminds us
that the satirist is fixed or tied to his subject, and is therefore
a valuable source of material on it. If satire is, as Edward W.
Rosenheim, Jr. asserts, *"an attack by means of a manifest
fiction upon discernible historic particulars,"*[6] then so much
the better for it as a revelatory art form. To the extent that
satire is explicitly social it is a valuable treasure of information on its subject—society.

I would say then that the distortions, caricatures, and
grotesques in Capp's satire do not lead us away from truths
about American society and American values, but instead are
means of leading us to them; the fictions lead us to reality.
In the following chapter I have a good deal to say about the
intellectual quality of Capp's satire, its mindfulness (rather

than mindlessness), and the particular devices he uses in creating what I would describe as a distinctively American satirical comic strip.[7]

II

Unlike Jay Gatsby, who sprang out of a Platonic conception of himself, Li'l Abner has quite a satirical genealogy. Descriptions of places similar to Dogpatch and characters like that in "Li'l Abner" are found in our earliest literature, and the use of the same techniques, the same character types, the same kind of language, and the same style in many earlier writers. Of course no writer put things together exactly the way Capp has, but the foundation was there for him to build on. And upon this native American base he has added a good dose of Yiddish humor, its attendant moralizing outlook, and its sense of fantasy.

In order to see how "Li'l Abner" has grown out of and utilized earlier American humor, it is best to characterize the strip, and then to compare it to similar works in American satire. I might add that it is quite difficult to encapsulate the strip, because it has been appearing for more than thirty years, has a very large number of characters, and has dealt with many subjects. However, I will now discuss certain fundamental aspects of "Li'l Abner," its setting, its most important characters, and its themes, in an effort to give a basis for comparison.

* * *

"Li'l Abner" is a satirical comic strip, created in 1934 by Al Capp.[8] It deals with the lives of a group of unusual characters who are residents of a mythical land, "Dogpatch," which Capp has described as "an average stone age community." It exists somewhere in America and is supposedly rural and hillbillylike.[9] The action in the strip, however, goes on all over America; often it takes place in big cities and sometimes in foreign lands, but much of the strip involves doings in Dogpatch.

The main characters in the strip are these:

Abner: The strip's hero, a big, handsome, dumb hillbilly with a strong back, a weak mind, and a great heart, who is, of course, taken advantage of by everyone.

The Yokums: Mammy Yokum and Pappy Yokum, Abner's mother and father. Mammy is a small "pipe-smoking runt" who is the strongest person in Dogpatch and, therefore, its social leader. Pappy Yokum is a weakling who is seldom of any importance in the stories.[10]

Daisy Mae: Abner's wife, who chased him for many years and finally married him. He had made an oath to do whatever his hero, Fearless Fosdick, did—and Fosdick got married.

Fearless Fosdick: the hero of a cartoon strip that appears within "Li'l Abner"; he is a parody of the famous comic strip detective hero, Dick Tracy.

There are other secondary characters, such as Tiny Yokum (Abner's fifteen-and-a-half year old brother), Honest Abe Yokum (Abner's son), Salomey (a pig), and other representative types, grotesques, and symbolic creations, about whom I shall have more to say later.

Capp describes his characters as "broad burlesques" in the tradition of his ideals—Rube Goldberg, F. C. Opper, Milt Gross, and Maurice Ketten—and as "innocents . . . surrounded by a world of superaverage people." He says:

> This innocence of theirs is indestructible so that while they possess all the homely virtues in which we profess to believe, they seem ingenuous because the

world around them is irritated by them, cheats them, kicks them around. They are trusting, kind, loyal, generous and patriotic. . . . Of course, what they don't know is that it takes more than innocence to be truly virtuous —but that's another story.

If a point of view can be called anything as neat as a formula, mine for writing "Li'l Abner" is to throw comedy characters into melodramatic situations in a simple-minded way.[11]

I think Capp's description of his "formula" is a bit disarming and oversimplified. While he often uses simple characters, each of whom generally represents the equivalent of a Jonsonian "humour," Capp's fascination with the symbolic, wit, and satire tend to produce what I call "harmonics," rich levels of meaning and humor that move beyond the limited scope of the original creations.[12]

At this point, I would like to say something about Capp's favorite subjects and the range of the strip. A partial catalogue of the episodes in "Li'l Abner" reveals that the following professions and subjects are typical targets for Capp's satire:

PROFESSIONS	SUBJECTS
businessman	business
lawyer	politics
psychiatrist	popular culture
politician	love
policeman	courtship
artist	marriage
writer	fads
janitor	news items
cook	fashion
gangster	

PROFESSIONS
salesman
doctor
nurse
entertainer
celebrity

It might be noted that the most frequent subjects for Capp involve love, marriage, and the family—or what might be called courtship and its consequences—and business and politics. And, I might add, even courtship is socialized, turned into a community event. What we find then, and we should expect this, is that Capp's concerns are social or public.

Capp has this wide range precisely *because* he is functioning as a comic artist, and is not forced to abide by the limitations imposed upon the tragedies. As Wylie Sypher says:

> The coherent plot is vital to tragic theatre (Aristotle says that plot is the very soul of tragedy) ; and a tragic action needs to convey a sense of destiny, inevitability, and foreordination. . . . The fate of a tragic hero needs o be made "intelligible" as a comic hero's fate does not; or at least tragic fate has the force of "necessity" even if it is not "intelligible." . . . Comedy, on the contrary, can freely yield its action to surprise, chance, and all the changes in fortune that fall outside the necessities of tragic myth, and can present "character" for its own sake.[13]

He puts this another way when he says that comedy "admits the disorderly into the realm of art."[14] It is because of the possibilities in the comic that many now see it as something not "opposed" to tragedy but somehow "beyond" it.[15]

Capp's comic plots do involve conflicts, but they are not

always as simple as Capp would have us believe. Often we are left with confused resolutions and ironies, such as the conclusion to Capp's *Return of the Shmoo*,[16] in which Abner ends the book saying: "No Shmoos left!! Now, everybody can go back to working hard, paying taxes—and being terrified o' war!! —in other words—HAPPY DAYS ARE HERE AGAIN!!"

This ironical conclusion, aside from its very obvious humor, does not leave us with the ease, the sense of well being, that we should have in a simple contest between good and evil forces or characters.

Capp employs a number of devices to create humor. Aside from his fantastic characters, he uses dialect, he injects a great deal of action into his plots, he gives people strange names, he makes many puns and is often rather witty. Also, he employs irony and ridicules famous people with wild caricatures. I will have a more comprehensive discussion of Capp's humor later and will enlarge upon this quick sketch of the strip. For the moment, however, what I have done is enough to give an idea of the strip which, I hope, will enable me to point out how Abner is a representative figure in American satire.

III

There is a very early work in American literature that has such remarkable similarities to "Li'l Abner" that I am almost led to believe that it has influenced Capp. I have in mind certain passages from the writings of William Byrd, one of our earliest literary figures of any consequence and interest, who lived between 1674 and 1744, had a library of more than 3,600 titles, and was very rich.

Byrd discusses life in North Carolina, mentioning a

place called "Lubberland" where, due to the climate, the "easiness of raising provisions, and the slothfulness of the people,"[17] life has a rather unusual quality. Lubberland might well be a prototype of Dogpatch. The similarities continue: The Lubberlanders have a drink called "bombo" which may be the counterpart of a drink called "Kickapoo Joy Juice" that is sometimes found in "Li'l Abner." Byrd also mentions the one major problem the Lubberlanders face:

> . . . very often, in autumn, when the apples begin to ripen, they are visited with numerous flights of para-queets, that bite all the fruit to pieces in a moment, for the sake of the kernels. The havoc they make is some-times so great, that whole orchards are laid waste in spite of all the noises that can be made. . . .[18]

This is somewhat similar to the situation in Dogpatch, where the sole industry is turnips, and where every year the turnips are attacked by turnip-crazy termites, just a few hours before harvest. I would not push these parallels, however, because Byrd's work, in turn, is based upon certain conventions in humor: namely, that agrarian types are crude, eat food that is coarse and limited, are addicted to strange drinks, and have very odd customs.

The roots of "Li'l Abner" are also found in works of writers commonly called "Southwestern humorists," writers such as Augustus Longstreet, George Washington Harris, T. B. Thorpe, and Johnson Hooper, who were popular in the 1830's, a hundred years before "Li'l Abner" first appeared. Their works can be characterized as having a fairly accurate rendering of colloquial speech, a considerable amount of exaggeration and fantasy, much distortion, and certain "mythic" implications. Capp makes a number of changes but still draws upon them a good deal, especially in his use of dialect and character.

Probably the most easily recognizable characteristic of this Southwestern humor is the language, which is often very creatively manipulated. These humorists took evident delight in the vernacular, but they were also quite inventive—creating words of their own, playing with dialect, and employing idiosyncratic spelling.

George Washington Harris, for example, used misspellings (or phonetic spelling) in his Sut Lovingood tales. In the "Rare Ripe Garden Seed" we find:

> Well, es I wer sayin, mam wer feedin us brats ontu mush an' milk, wifout the milk, an' es I wer the baby then, she hilt me so es tu see that I got my sheer. Whar thar ain't enuf feed, big childer roots littil childer outen the troff, an' gobbils up thar part.[19]

The hillbilly characters in "Li'l Abner" speak in a somewhat similar manner. The following is typical of Abner's speech: "KIGMIES IS WONDIFUL!! When yo gits foorious at somebody—YO KICKS A KIGMY!! THET takes all th' ANGER outa YO'—an', as fo th' Kigmy—HE jest plain LOVES it!!"[20]

In T. B. Thorpe's "The Big Bear of Arkansas" we find exaggeration and invented words as well as dialect:

> "The season for bar hunting, stranger," said the man of Arkansaw, "is generally all the year round, and the hunts take place about as regular. I read in history that varmints have their fat season, and their lean season. That is not the case in Arkansaw, feeding as they do upon the *spontenacious* productions of the sile, they have one continued fat season the year round: though in winter things in this way is rather more greasy than in summer, I must admit."[21]

Thorpe continues in the same manner and moves into the realm of the fantastic. Describing a bear he has "run" into a terrific sweat, Thorpe's hunter says:

> In this fix I blazed at him, and pitch me naked into a briar patch if the steam didn't come out of the bullet-hole ten foot in a straight line. The fellow, I reckon, was made on the high-pressure system, and the lead sort of bit his biler. . . . I have no doubt if he had kept on two miles farther his insides would have been stewed; and I expect to meet with a varmint yet of extra bottom, who will run himself into a skinful of bar's grease: it is possible, much onliklier things have happened.[22]

The same type of bravura and exaggeration is to be found in Capp. Here is Marryin' Sam's description of the eight-dollar wedding:

> Fust—Ah strips t' th' waist, an' rassles th' four biggest guests!! Next—a fast demon-stray-shun o' how t' cheat yore friends at cards!!—follyed by four snappy jokes—guaranteed t' embarrass man or beast—an'—then after ah dances a jig wif a pig, Ah yanks out two o' mah teeth, an' presents 'em t' th' bride an' groom—as mementos o' th' occasion!!—then—Ah really gits goin!!—Ah offers t' remove any weddin' guest's appendix, wif mah bare hands—free!! Then yo' spread-eagles me, fastens mah arms an' laigs t' four wild jackasses—an'—bam!! yo' fires a gun!!—While they tears me t' pieces—Ah puffawms th' weddin' ceremony!![23]

The big bear that Thorpe wrote about, who is generally held to be the great-grandfather of Faulkner's bear, has a mythic quality. He is described as an *"unhuntable bar,"* who *"died when his time come,"* which suggests that the bear had some dimension beyond the ordinary. The subject of myth is very controversial. I am using the term in a rather loose manner, taking it to mean "a purely fictitious narrative usually involving supernatural persons, actions, or events, and embodying some popular idea concerning natural or historical phenomena." This definition comes from the *Oxford English Dictionary* and is quoted in *A Dictionary of American-English Usage.* Myth is sometimes held to deal with the doings of the gods, in contrast to folklore, which deals with people, but the distinction tends to become blurred when there are god-like people, "creation" animals, and the like.[24] According to Daniel G. Hoffman, whose book *Form and Fable in American Fiction* is an important study of the influence of folk materials on the American literary imagination, "there is no general agreement even among professional scholars as to what folklore actually is."[25]

In a number of respects, "Li'l Abner," like the work of the Southwestern humorists, has a mythic quality. For one thing, Dogpatch itself is a mythical (i.e., fictitious) community located someplace in the United States. Many of the characters have rather special supernatural powers: Mammy Yokum has visions, Joe Btfsplk is an unfailing jinx, Ole Man Mose gives predictions which always come true, and Evil Eye Fleegle is master of a super-powerful force, the "whammy." There are a number of rather unusual creatures in the strip, such as the Shmoo, the Bald Iggle, and the Kigmy, which certainly embody elements of the mythic, and are the descendants of a number of fantastic animals associated with Paul Bunyan and American folklore. Long before Americans had heard of the Shmoo (which, after all, is a hybrid—an American-Yiddish beast), there were tales of Axehandle Hounds, Hangdowns, Squonks, and Tripoderos.

However, Capp makes some interesting variations on the *style* of the Southwestern humorists. The Southwestern humorists were Whigs and used their literary powers to champion conservative causes, while Capp, on the other hand, has been associated with New Deal liberalism. (Although Colton Waugh and others claim that Henry Wallace was the model upon whom Abner was based, he actually looks like Capp.) Also, Capp does not seem to 'burn" the way some of the Southwestern writers did; Kenneth Lynn describes Longstreet, for example, as a "fanatic."[26]

As far as literary style *per se* is concerned, the differences between the Southwestern humorists and Capp are quite revealing. Lynn suggests that, aside from the use of the vernacular, there are two devices common to the writings of these humorists: the "framed" story, in which the author introduces a character who then tells the story so that the reader gets it second-hand, so to speak; and the employment of a "Self-controlled Gentleman" as a literary hero. As Lynn puts it: "By now it should be clear why the literary hero developed by the Southwestern humorists was a Self-controlled Gentleman—[because he was] the very model of Whiggery's ideals."[27] and later: ". . . the frame device eventually became the structural trademark of Southwestern humor . . . because it suited so well the myth-making purposes of the humorists."[28]

There is implied within the very structure of the Southwestern humorous story a certain class bias. The doings of the lower class elements, the buffoons and rapscallions who are the protagonists of these tales, are always painted in relief against the normative figure of the "Self-controlled Gentleman." He is, so to speak, telling a joke on them, even if we sometimes find them sympathetic and appealing.

Mark Twain, according to Lynn, was the first to reverse this convention, by having the narrator tell the joke on himself. This change from a spectator's humor to a victim's humor was a major transformation in the treatment of the

American frontier. The frame was ultimately discarded and the ethos of the tales became much more democratic. Capp is following Mark Twain in his own adaptations of the conventions of Southwestern humor. It is quite obvious that Capp's humor is "victim" humor, though the strip has a decided "class bias." His hero is as far removed from the "Self-controlled Gentleman" as one can go.

Playing upon Capp's mind and affecting his technique we find two basic influences: the first is the influence of the various Southwestern humorists; the second is the influence of Jewish humor, which also is a "victim" humor. Capp uses Jewish words and Jewish terms for characters (or should we call them creations?) such as the Shmoo and a king named Nogoodnick, places such as the Gulf of Pincus, and so forth. His synthesis of two types of humor is, I think, one of the keys to the popularity of the strip.

There is an implicit (and often explicit) moralism to "Li'l Abner" which is typical of Jewish humor and of Jewish folktales. Angelo Rappoport, who has written *The Folklore of the Jews*, describes Jewish folklore in the following manner:

> Jewish folktales . . . differ in some respects from those of other nations, for whilst they may have originally been tales and recitals of an anecdotal character, invented for amusement only, an early form of romantic and imaginative literature, the unwritten fiction of the people, they invariably, as they are now recorded, have one purpose, viz., that of instructing and moralizing. Nearly all Jewish folktales either satirize presumption and pride, glorify piety and wisdom, or embody ancient Jewish traditions, beliefs, customs.[29]

For an example of this moralizing, there is a scene in the Kigmy adventure in which a murderer is in the death cell.

The guard comes in and the following conversation takes place:

PRISONER: I want a KIGMY! —one dat looks like ME!!

GUARD: HMPH!! —I thought you'd want one like th' judge that sentenced you—

PRISONER: NAH-H!! HE'S not to blame for me bein' here—th' only guy who IS t'blame is ME!! —for not going't' school, like my mudder told me!! —for hangin' around wit' that tough crowd she warned me AGAINST!! —For t'inkin' my mudder didn't know th' score, an' I did!! UMPH!! I richly DE-SERVE this!! (and he kicks the Kigmy.) [30]

Capp has disguised his moralizing with tough-guy dialect and humor, but the message is still there, and rather explicit too. The psychological implications of the whole Kigmy story are fascinating; and those of this scene, in which the prisoner kicks a facsimile of himself, particularly interesting.

There are several other important variations that Capp has made on Southwestern humor. Unlike Harris' Sut Lovingood, Abner is always shown to be one who lacks self-understanding, though both characters function as social critics. Abner doesn't seem to be aware that he is a fool; perhaps because he is so dumb. Sut *is* a fool but he realizes it. In the "Rare Ripe Garden-Seed" he says: "I'se mad at myself yet, fur rite thar I show'd the fust flash ove the nat'ral born durn fool what I now is."[31] Combined with his awareness of his foolishness is an awareness of what might be called "the problem of evil." His first scare has left what he calls "a scar ontu my thinkin works." Unlike Abner, he also has active sexual longings and unlike all comic strip characters he is anti-religious.

Abner's innocence, naivete, and complete trust in everyone force the reader to make judgments. Of course Capp leads him to these judgments, but they must be made by the reader as he watches Abner being initiated into the complexities of the world. Abner never catches on, and because of this, he always remains free to become involved in other adventures. He never is scarred and never learns. He also has no memory. He tends to bring into sharp focus the conflict between the decent people and the villains, and in so doing is almost a parody of the "Self-controlled gentleman." The normative figure, with whom the reader can sympathize but who certainly is no model for imitation, is a fool. We do not have a model of democracy's ideals and perhaps, through this stylistic device, Capp is saying we cannot. The only other figure who could possibly be described as normative would be Mammy Yokum, and she is generally used only as a *Deus ex Machina*, to get Abner out of impossibly tight situations. I will have more to say about Pansy, the "Mother God" figure, later.

IV

In being far removed from the "Self-controlled Gentleman," Abner immediately suggests the influence of Cervantes' Don Quixote, who was a gentleman without self control. There are a number of reasons to think that Abner is a modernized, adapted version of the picaresque. In the following analysis I am indebted to Robert Alter's study of the picaresque novel, *Rogue's Progress*.[32] Alter suggests that the following points are typical of the picaresque:

1. He accepts the world as it is, and is not a rebel, even though he is somewhat of an "outcast."

2. He is a "servant of many masters."

3. His position as an outsider allows him to observe society and take advantage of it in many respects, "without being concerned with many of the demands that society makes on the individuals belonging to it."

4. There is no logical conclusion to a picaresque novel. All one can do is break it off.

5. The picaroon, scapegrace though he may be, is also, like the traditional hero, a child of the gods: despite all the troubles he gets himself into, he is never seriously hurt and never perceptibly tainted.

6. There are two types of picaroons: the "master of his fate" who tends to be something of a deceiver and rogue, and the "butt of fortune," who is a "man of many adversities, . . . never allowed rest or security."

7. The virtues of the picaresque hero are those of the heart, not of the head.

8. He functions as a touchstone for the virtues of others.

It seems obvious that Li'l Abner represents the "butt of fortune" tradition in the picaresque, and fits Alter's description of one kind of picaresque hero quite well. He may not be a servant in the most literal sense, but he is generally in the employment of somebody—generally some unscrupulous person whose schemes he inadvertently foils. In being innocent and dumb, he is able to function in society without responsibilities that normally would be his, and despite all the dangers and fantastic adventures he has, he is never harmed. And, as in all comic strips, his adventures never have a real conclusion. In fact, the average comic strip continues even after the death of the originator. Another artist is found to imitate the style of the original one, and the strip continues. While all comic strips have the episodic structure of the picaresque, most of them do not have the other elements. As a form, the comic strip is not really a modernization of the picaresque. In "Li'l Abner" the picaresque qualities come not from the form but from Capp's imaginative use of a literary tradition.

V

There is another tradition upon which Capp draws that is of some interest to us as we pursue the relationship between the way style affects "content" and emerges as *meaning*, and that is the grotesque. It is extremely difficult to define "the grotesque," but clearly it involves such matters as distortions, caricature, and overstatement, incongruity, unnaturalness, and ugliness. For Sherwood Anderson, grotesques were people whose espousal of single truths led to distorted views of reality. Sypher sees it as a means of elevating "hatred into art." In Capp's use of the grotesque, in his drawings and narratives, he goes back to ancient Greek comedy, where the grotesque was very popular. But he is also very dependent upon the type of writing done by Ben Jonson, who enunciated his theory of "humours" and laid the foundation for the modern use of grotesques. It is the grotesque and its attendant specters that William Van O'Connor finds as typical of American literature. He says: "Our writers are terribly preoccupied with the irrational, the unpredictable, the bizarre, with the grotesque;"[33] he sees the grotesque in the work of Poe, Crane, Norris, the "southern school," Anderson, and West.

O'Connor's discussion of West is of special interest:

Nathanael West once wrote that he had based the technique of *Miss Lonelyhearts* on the comic strip. "Each chapter," he wrote, "instead of going forward in time, goes backward, forwards, up and down in space like a picture." West's mention of the comic strip is an important clue to the peculiar nature of his stylization. The characters are one dimensional. Each represents one thing only, tends to be obsessed, and moves through the action with the sort of inertia common to comic strips.[34]

We see that the very form of the comic strip has affected the sensibility of one of our most gifted writers. If the flatness and one-dimensionality of the comic strip character is sometimes a liability, it can also be an asset, for it facilitates compression, exaggeration, and stylization. We suspend our disbelief all the more willingly—yet, as West's work shows, even with limited, one-dimensional characters, great art is possible.

O'Connor's conclusion is also noteworthy:

Modern literature has heightened and stylized the antipoetic and the ugly. The grotesque, as a genre or a form of modern literature, simultaneously confronts the antipoetic and the ugly and presents them, when viewed out of the side of the eye, as the closest we can come to the sublime. The grotesque affronts our sense of established order and satisfies, or partly satisfies, our need for at least a tentative, a more flexible ordering.[35]

What we find then is that the grotesque, as a stylistic device, contains a *built-in* criticism of society. Apart from any didactic message it may or may not have, apart from the specific nature of any adventures in which the characters may be involved, it is by its very form, a critique of the social order.

Of course a logical question now arises. If comic strips are filled with characters who are "grotesques" by definition, why emphasize the grotesques in "Li'l Abner"? The answer to this involves a further elaboration of the term grotesque. To the degree that comic strip characters, in general, are one-dimensional, they are grotesque. But in "Li'l Abner," as in certain other comics, there is a conscious attempt at distortion. We find this both in the drawings of characters and in their personalities. Capp uses representational types in his work—that is, his Senator Phogbound is meant to typify *all* politicians, and the same applies to Capp's businessmen and other characters. Thus, while in the comic strip form we cannot find rounded three-dimensional characters we can, very easily, find symbolic types—or perhaps stereotypes. If we lose individual characters, we gain symbols—which means that for our purposes we still have a good deal to work with.

I have just suggested that the grotesque, as a stylistic device, is, in itself, a criticism of society. But it is possible to say even more about this criticism. Thomas Mann sees it as inherently anti-bourgeois: ". . . if I may say so, the grotesque is the genuine anti-bourgeois style; and however bourgeois Anglo-Saxondom may otherwise be or appear, it is a fact that in art the comic-grotesque has always been its strong point."[36]

If Mann is correct and the grotesque style is an anti-bourgeois style, then Capp could not have been wiser in adopting it for his purposes. He says, in the preface to *From Dogpatch to Slobbovia*, that he aims to "create suspicion of, and disrespect for, the perfection of all established institutions." But Capp's main target seems to me what might be called bourgeois smugness, narrowness, and hypocrisy, at which he flails away with fury.

A point that David Worcester makes is relevant here. He sees the function of the grotesque as "dislocating absolute standards and shocking men into an awareness of the relativity of things,"[37] and says:

> By making us accept an eccentric, or grotesque, scale of values in opposition to our normal scale, the author

67

creates positive and negative poles. Across the gap leaps
the spark of irony. The secret of detail in grotesque
satire is that its ultimate appeal is to ideas.[38]

We see that in his use of the grotesque, Capp is not at all
mindless, and I would suggest that there is in fact, a good
deal of *mind* in "Li'l Abner." Capp's use of the grotesque
gives him a built-in defense, so to speak, which allows him
to analyze society and point out its absurdities, yet "get away
with it."

There is another tie-in between the comic strip and
American literary style. Fry has expressed a theory of the
comic strip as romance:

The essential element of plot in romance is adventure,
which means that romance is naturally a sequential and
processional form, hence we know it better from fiction
than drama. At its most naive it is an endless form in
which a central character who never develops or ages
goes through one adventure after another until the
author himself collapses. We see this form in comic
strips, where the central characters persist for years in
a state of refrigerated deathlessness.[39]

This is a most interesting statement in view of the current
tendency on the part of many literary scholars to see the
romance, rather than the novel, as basic to the American
literary tradition.[40] If this is true then it shows that American popular culture reflects, more than we might suspect,
the stylistic conventions of "serious" literature, and suggests
that, as a *form,* the comic-strip is very much an *American*
idiom.

VI

Capp has said that among his ideals in the realm of
comic strip artistry are Rube Goldberg, Frederick B. Opper,

and Milt Gross. He has been influenced by them, both in his graphic style and in his general approach to comic-strip humor.

Capp draws on all three in his use of wacky characters, in his employment of the grotesque, and in his manipulation of satire. Like Goldberg and Gross, he uses Yiddish humor and relatively sexy women who are somewhat realistically drawn (though many or most of the other characters are comic and caricatures). Goldberg has a character, "Uncle Clumsy McNutt," who is a representative type—an American variant of the Schlemiel. In Yiddish humor a Schlemiel is someone who invariably spills soup on people and is always making mistakes. Nathan Ausubel defines him as "a clumsy bungler, an inept person."[41] He is the same type of character that Capp has created in Joe Btfsplk, Uncle Future Yokum, and Evil-Eye Fleegle.

I would characterize the influence of these comic strips artists on Capp as "general" or "temperamental." That is, I do not think he used specific things taken from these cartoonists so much as he adopted their approach—irreverent, whimsical, and satirical. His graphic style has also been influenced by Ham Fisher, for whom Capp once worked.[42] Abner's body is now quite similar to that of Fisher's hero, Joe Palooka. The combination that Capp has made from all these elements has led, I think, to a strip that is quite original, and a style that is unique.

Narrative Technique
and The Meaning of Form

I

I have already commented upon my informing conception of style as having, so to speak, a "content" of its own. In the forthcoming chapters on narration, dialogue, and graphic technique, I shall enlarge upon and develop this idea. In this chapter I hope to show that Capp's narrative technique uses the conventions of satire, and that even in the way it treats subjects of particular interest to Americans it reveals something about American society and character.[1]

Earlier I mentioned that the very nature of most of the books dealing with popular culture shows that we find it hard to come to grips with it. The same applies to comics in general, and to "Li'l Abner" in particular. There is much disagreement over the matter of how comics should be classified and it is hard to be other than arbitrary. For example, Colton Waugh puts "Li'l Abner" in a category called "Hemen, Hail," but Martin Sheridan classifies "Li'l Abner" as an adventure strip, and it is possible to think of it as a family strip also. All the confusions are centered around a lack of agreement as to what is the best *basis* for classification: subject matter, audience, style, and so forth. But choosing a basis is dependent upon what is to be done and since very few people know what they want to do with the comics (other than wrap fish), the problem becomes even more confusing. For my purposes, the best way to classify "Li'l Abner" is on the basis of its style. One aspect of style is narrative technique. The stories in "Li'l Abner" conform remarkably well to the narrative conventions of the satiric tale.

For purposes of analysis I have selected what appear to be representative and important episodes in the strip. I have tried to include in my discussion the famous symbolic "creations" such as the Kigmy and the Shmoo, and the most important characters. In addition, I have compared earlier and later episodes in order to see whether Capp's style and attitudes have changed and developed. I have paid particular attention to the four collections of Capp's work that have appeared: *The Life and Times of the Shmoo, The Return of the Shmoo, The World of Li'l Abner,* and most recently, *From Dogpatch to Slobbovia.*

I shall begin by analyzing the narrative technique of the seven stories in *From Dogpatch to Slobbovia,* in which Capp's own comments reveal his satiric intentions. Each story is briefly described below, along with the explanation of its resolution and its source of humor.

Story and Resolution	Source of Humor
1. New residents of Dogpatch are not well-received because of their square eyes. Mammy discovers that square eyed people are just like everyone else and forces the community to accept them.	1. Square eyes. Comic invention used for social criticism.
2. Evil-Eye Fleegle, jilted by his girl friend for an astronaut, puts a whammy on the sun, turns his eyeballs inside out, and petrifies himself. Mammy gets Fleegle to return to life, take his whammy off the sun, and save the world from burning up.	2. Exaggeration and creation of grotesque characters.
3. A futuroid camera takes pictures of the future which show dire things for Abner. Everything that Abner does to prevent the things foretold by the camera actually helps them come true.	3. Irony. Abner outwits himself and finally destroys camera which has, however, predicted its own end.
4. Abner inherits Kig-	4. Creation of Kigmy as

STORY AND RESOLUTION

SOURCE OF HUMOR

mies, masochistic animals that love to be kicked. They threaten to break up the composure of society (which is shown to be based upon meanness, malice, etc.) until they discover how nice it is to kick people, rather than to be kicked. Mammy sends them back to Australia.

masochist - aggression victim and change of Kigmy into aggressor.

5. General Bullmoose makes a fortune by exploiting human gullibility and stupidity. He buys worthless land and then sells it back at a great profit because people assume there must have been a legitimate reason for his having bought the land. The Slobbovians get the money to buy their land back by exploiting the Cold War rivalry.

5. Revelation of human stupidity and demonstration that governments can be as silly as individuals.

6. Pappy eats an egg that threatens to destroy the

6. Logic. Reader can predict consequences of

Source of Humor	Story and Resolution
world. Abner ridicules his father's claim that he has saved the world, though it happens to be true.	situation in which birds lay eggs twice their size, then die. Unless the chain of events is stopped (by eating the egg), the world is doomed.
7. Lower Slobbovian children, after years of being terrified by a hairy creature that comes visiting them on Christmas, discover that he has been trying to visit them because he loves them, not because he wanted to hurt them. He becomes the Slobbovian equivalent of Santa Claus.	7. Irony. What is expected or held to be true (for very insubstantial reasons) is shown to be false; people as slaves to uncritical custom are ridiculed.

Several generalizations can be made about these stories. For one thing, there is a considerable amount of *inventiveness* in the formation of somewhat grotesque characters and of unusual creatures such as the Kigmy. Also, the stories are all rather direct. There are few subplots although some of the stories have more than one episode; thus the long stories tend to be a series of short episodes that are joined together. Capp does, of course, have his celebrated "Fearless Fosdick" strip-within-a-strip elsewhere, but for the most part each story is direct and simple. In addition, some of the stories have no real comic resolution. In the sixth story, for example, Abner doesn't believe Pappy's story about having saved the world by eating an egg. It is a straight story that has no trick ending and is typical of Capp's resolutions. Many times he ends stories by having Abner read "Fearless Fosdick." At other times he relies on clever verbal gimmicks as, for example, in one story (in *The World of Li'l Abner*) in which a jackass hauls Abner across the finishing line in a Sadie Hawkins Day race. Abner is about to be married to the owner of the jackass when Mammy intervenes and reminds everyone of the rules, which say that whoever drags a person over the line has the right to marry him. All the jackass can say is "neigh" so Abner is saved, thanks to a literal interpretation of the letter, not the spirit, of the law.

It can also be seen that Capp is fascinated by *ironic* situations—and by all kinds of conflicts of opposites. In *From Dogpatch to Slobbovia*, for example, we have many "reversals": the square eyes of the people, Evil-Eye Fleegle turning his eyeballs inside out, the Kigmies changing from kick-loving to love-kicking beasts, and the Snowman becoming a loved rather than a hated creature. We also find the Slobbovians buying back land which they have sold and Abner making the futuroid's predictions come true in trying to frustrate them. Every story in the book is ironic. Capp also capitalizes upon the paradoxes that arise when verbal opposites "confront each other." In a Shmoo adventure he has signs proclaiming "Shmoos are bad—because they're good."[2] His use of paradox suggests a relatively complex approach to experience: it involves more than simple problems and simple solutions.

There is a good deal of richness to the characterization because though the characters tend to be monomaniacs, grotesques pursuing their "single truths," many of them function symbolically, as I have said, and add a dimension of meaning to the stories. A distinction should be made, also, between the *nature* of a character and his *function*. That is, a relatively simple character may function in a complex manner—as a symbol or a social type. Also, there are often several ways of looking at the characters. Some people see Abner as a hero, others as a fool; Bullmoose is a money-mad businessman who is a stereotype of *the* businessman, Senator Phogbound is a caricature of the politician, and so on. And these caricatures and grotesques contain, as I have suggested, built-in criticisms of society, and are much more involved than they might seem. Frye makes a similar point in *Anatomy of Criticism*:

> . . . the sentimental notion of an antithesis between the lifelike character and the stock type is a vulgar error. All lifelike characters whether in drama or fiction, owe their consistency to the appropriateness of the stock type which belongs to their dramatic function.[3]

To make what I have been talking about more evident, I will reproduce one of Capp's more celebrated stories and use it to discuss his narrative technique. The following episode is taken from the collection *The World of Li'l Abner* and is a satire on zoot-suits.

II

This episode can be broken down into three main parts: (1) There is an introduction, in which the main characters —the zoot-suit clothes manufacturers and their dupe, Abner —are presented and the plot is begun. (2) In the middle, the action is developed—in this case, the zoot-suit mania is shown as having taken over the country, and tension is built up. What will happen to America? Will the conservative-cut

CHAPTER THREE

"ZOOT SUIT" YOKUM

Zoot-Suit Yokum Episode

80

81

83

ENTIRE NATION GRIPPED
BY ZOOT-SUIT MANIA!!

ZOOT-SUIT YOKUM

FROM MAINE TO CALIFORNIA A FANATICAL TYPE OF HERO-WORSHIP HAS ENGULFED THIS ONCE CONSERVATIVE NATION. THE OBJECT OF ALL THIS ADULATION IS "ZOOT-SUIT YOKUM" WHO HAS, UPON INNUMERABLE OCCASIONS, RUSHED TO SCENES OF DISASTER ALL OVER THE COUNTRY — AND, WITH INCREDIBLE, FOOLHARDY COURAGE, PERFORMED AMAZING FEATS OF STRENGTH AND HEROISM. NATURALLY, "ZOOT-SUIT YOKUM" HAS BECOME THE IDOL OF ALL RED-BLOODED YOUNG AMERICANS — AND THIS IDOL-WORSHIP HAS LED MILLIONS OF MEN TO IMITATE HIS PECULIAR COSTUME, KNOWN AS THE "ZOOT SUIT." CLOTHING STORES REPORT THAT THERE HAS BEEN A MAD RUSH TO BUY "ZOOT SUITS" — WHILE THE REGULAR MEN'S CLOTHING MARKET HAS HIT ITS WORST SLUMP IN ONE HUNDRED YEARS.

A PHOTO FROM A DAILY NEWSPAPER!!

ZOOT SUITS OR NOTHING!

WE'LL WALK AROUND LIKE THIS UNTIL OUR LOCAL MERCHANTS STOCK UP WITH ZOOT SUITS!

A ZOOT SUIT FOR EVERY MAN OR BUST!

IRATE CITIZENS PICKET CLOTHING STORES!!

GOVERNOR ISSUES ORDER BANNING ZOOT-SUIT WEARERS!!

CONSIDERS ZOOT SUIT A THROWBACK TO BARBARISM - AND A PUBLIC EYESORE!

GOVERNOR IMPEACHED!!

INDIGNANT GROUP OF LEGISLATORS WHO TODAY IMPEACHED THE GOVERNOR!!

WIFE KILLS HUSBAND!!

"HE REFUSED TO WEAR A ZOOT SUIT" - SHE SAYS!! "I'M GLAD I SHOT HIM THROUGH THE HEAD SIX TIMES!!"

GOES ON TRIAL TOMORROW!!

JURY UNANIMOUSLY ACQUITS WIFE WHO KILLED ZOOT-SUIT HATING HUSBAND!

"WHAT'S SO HATEFUL ABOUT ZOOT SUITS?" ASKS JURY FOREMAN!!!

NON-ZOOT-SUIT WEARER RIDDEN OUT OF TOWN ON RAIL !!

INDIGNANT CITIZENS TAKE LAW INTO OWN HANDS WHEN FELLOW-TOWNSMAN REFUSES TO CO-OPERATE IN BEAUTIFYING TOWN BY WEARING ZOOT-SUIT !!

ZOOT-SUIT YOKUM OFFERED NOMINATION FOR PRESIDENCY IN 1944 !!

THIRD PARTY FORMED, TO BE KNOWN AS "THE ZOOT-SUIT PROGRESSIVES."

ELECTION SEEN CERTAIN !!

THE CONSERVATIVE CLOTHING MANUFACTURERS CALL A MEETING —

IF THIS ZOOT SUIT FEVER CONTINUES UNABATED, WE'LL ALL BE RUINED !!

WE'VE GOT TO FIGURE OUT SOME WAY TO MAKE MEN BUY CONSERVATIVE, SENSIBLE CLOTHES AGAIN !!

GENTLEMEN! — THE IDEA OF "ZOOT-SUIT YOKUM" WAS CREATED BY THE GREAT "IDEA" MAN, J. COLOSSAL McGENIUS, WHO CHARGES $10,000 A WORD FOR ADVICE !! —

IF HE CREATED "ZOOT-SUIT YOKUM" FOR THE ZOOT SUIT MANUFACTURERS, PERHAPS HE CAN FIGURE OUT A WAY OF DESTROYING HIM — FOR US !! IT'LL COST $10,000 A WORD — BUT IT'LL BE WORTH IT !!

MR. McGENIUS, I REPRESENT THE ASSOCIATION OF CONSERVATIVE CLOTHING MANUFACTURERS !

I'M GLAD TO MEET YOU !

(— "HMM !— WOULD "I'M" BE CONSIDERED ONE OR TWO WORDS ?—? OH, WELL — I'LL MAKE IT TWO WORDS. THAT'S $60,000, ALREADY!)

88

clothes manufacturers all be destroyed? Will Zoot-Suit Yo-kum be elected president on the Zoot-Suit Progressive ticket? (3) Everything is quickly resolved in the conclusion. The image of Zoot-Suit Yokum as a hero is destroyed by the conservative clothes manufacturers, who discredit Yokum by using his double, a convict named Gat Garson, to do terrible things. When Zoot-Suit Yokum falls into unwarranted disgrace, the whole zoot-suit bubble collapses.

Capp's use of this rather straightforward three-part makeup shows a slight debt to the theater, and his compression and simplicity, to the short story. His little episodes are short, but they are not structured like the typical short story —at least as M. H. Abrams has characterized it. Abrams says that unlike the novelist, the short story writer

> usually begins the story close to, or even at, the climax, minimizes both exposition and the details of setting, keeps the complication down, often, to a single episode, and clears up the denouement quickly—sometimes in a sentence or two.[4]

This structuring is not typical of Capp. His stories almost always have some kind of introduction, a middle, and in this like most short stories generally a rather abrupt ending. This quick resolution is necessary because of the nature of the comic strip. It is difficult to sustain interest in installments, so once the story is resolved, the complications must be quickly cleared up and a new story started.

The characters in this story—except for McGenius' secretary—are all grotesques and eccentrics of one sort or another. The zoot-suiters wear fantastic clothing; McGenius charges ten thousand dollars for every word of advice; the Harvard man is an ape; Abner is the stupidest person in the world; the leader of the conservative clothing manufacturers is bald, has a great big nose, and is a freak; and all the minor characters are grotesques. There is hardly any middle-range here; everyone is either rich or poor, zoot-suiter or conservative, genius or moron. Only Abner is normative and he is shown to be a good-willed dupe without any brainpower.

Capp's use of these characters provides him with a safe way of criticizing society, and it is quite obvious that Abner functions the same way that Huck Finn does: he provides his creator with a character who cannot himself be criticized for his criticism. David Worcester, in *The Art of Satire*, says that the "satirist must simultaneously appear amiable to his audience, hostile to his enemies,"[5] and Abner is Capp's way of doing this.

Actually, Abner functions in a number of different ways, so that it is hard to classify him. This probably explains why he has been seen in so many different roles: fool, hero, superman, chump, and greenhorn.[6] A study made by one researcher on how Abner has been categorized says:

> The most frequent ones were: simpleton (22 per cent), chump or easily taken advantage of (20 per cent), superman or dragonslayer (16 per cent), heroic or admirable (12 per cent), greenhorn (12 per cent), a butt always getting the worst of it (7 per cent), idealist or romanticist (6 per cent), clumsy fool (5 per cent).[7]

While this study was made on a rather small sampling of students and is not entirely reliable, it does, at least, suggest that Abner is not easily pegged. People generally see him as a fool—because of the things he says and does—but they are not quite sure what kind of fool he is.

According to Sypher there are two kinds (he uses the word "order") of fools: the natural fool and the artificial fool. As he explains it:

> The natural fool is the archaic victim who diverts the wrath of the gods from the anointed figure of the king. He is the alter ego of the Successful Man who needs to exempt himself from the jealousy and ill will of the Olympians and who therefore provides himself with someone insolent or ignorant whom the gods smite.[8]

He is considerably different from the artificial fool, of which there are many different types, such as the seer, or the "voice crying in the wilderness." At his worst, "the artificial fool may be the parasite of old Greco-Roman comedies, a servile instrument in the hands of wealth and power."[9]

The curious thing that we notice is that in the strip Abner many times seems to be an artificial fool, but that he functions, for the reader, as a natural fool. Abner is very often a servile instrument of the rich and powerful. He is, as I pointed out in my discussion of Abner as a picaresque hero, "the servant of many masters." He works for the zoot-suit industry as "Zoot-Suit Yokum," he becomes Roundheels' bodyguard, and also works as a bodyguard for Rockwell B. Squeezeblood, head of the Squeezeblood comic strip syndicate, to mention just a few of his jobs.

We can distinguish three different aspects of Abner's role: first, his *role* is that of fool, generally (or often) an artificial fool, in the employ of the rich and powerful; second, he *functions, for the reader*, as a victim who diverts the wrath of the gods (and, who makes the reader feel better by being so obviously a stupid and inferior person) ; third, he is *a tool who allows Capp to judge society*. The criterion here is Abner's function; in the strip, for the reader, and for Capp. The biggest joke of all, of course, is that just as the reader laughs at Abner, his inferior, Abner laughs at the reader—and exposes his folly.

This can be seen even more clearly when we understand

that the fool is almost always alienated, set apart from society. As Sypher points out:

> . . . he is the detached spectator who has been placed, or has placed himself, outside accepted codes. From this point "outside,"—this extrapolated fulcrum—he takes his leverage on the rest of us, and from his point of vantage can exclaim with Puck, the comic avenger, "Lord, what fools these mortals be."[10]

When Abner makes the reader judge society, then he makes him judge himself, for he (the reader) is part of society. And Capp can laugh at everyone.

The remarkable thing about Abner is that somehow he does not become debased. Unlike Capp's other victims, who become as depraved as their ravishers, Abner maintains his basic goodness and incorruptibility, despite his occasional role as an unknowing "parasite".

It must also be noted that aside from the good-willed Abner, everyone in this adventure and almost everything brought up is shown in a decidedly negative light. The public is shown to be fickle and gullible; the expert is shown to have no sense of loyalty—he sells his information to anyone, and his advice, which built up the zoot-suit craze, leads to its destruction; the zoot-suit manufacturers are corrupt—they make millions and Abner makes eight dollars a week; heroism is shown to be foolhardy and abused—put to work for commercial gain; the conservative-clothes manufacturers are shown to be scoundrels—using Abner's double, Gat Garson, to destroy zoot-suitism. It is a very pessimistic commentary on human nature and society.

The characterization and the nature of the story indicate that we are to see it as a fantasy. The logic is ridiculously simple: man is posited to be a hero-imitating animal, which, while somewhat true, is obviously terribly unsatisfactory, reductionistic human psychology. But though the psychology is evidently absurd, the story is wonderfully consistent and logical. When Capp takes his psychology and applies it to subjects like politics and justice, the result is quite obviously madness.

There is, in addition, not the slightest concern with the probable, and we are forced to suspend the critical faculty which insists upon a satisfactory explanation for all acts. Abner functions as a superhuman type—he jumps in and out of mines, captures wildcats, and so forth. Once the image of Zoot-Suit Yokum as a hero is tarnished, the whole zoot-suit industry collapses with astonishing speed.

Everything is askew: the characters are all vicious eccentrics; human psychology is twisted and grossly oversimplified; the laws of physics are suspended; only the laws of logic hold. This establishes a tension. We are caught between belief and disbelief, and no matter what we do the results are unsatisfactory. The characters and their values are obviously unacceptable, their acts have little credibility, and the laws of cause and effect do not seem operative. Yet the logic leads to perversions of justice and decency.

The narrative here reinforces my description of "Li'l Abner" as a satire, for the form is very similar to that described by Highet in *The Anatomy of Satire*. Discussing the structure of satiric stories and plays he says:

> If they are long, they are usually episodic. Although the satirist pretends to be telling a continuous story and gives his fiction a single unifying title, he is less interested in developing a plot, with preparation, suspense, and climax, than in displaying many different aspects of an idea; and as a satirist, he does not believe the world is orderly and rational. Therefore gaps and interrup-

tions, even inconsistencies, in the story scarcely concern him. His characters flit from one amusing humiliation to another with scarcely any intervals of time and reflection. Seldom do they develop by degrees, as people in real novels do.[11]

He mentions that satiric tales often are both improbable and impossible and are based upon a suspension of belief. This also applies to the characters who "suffer more trials and tribulations than any ordinary man could endure without breaking down, going mad, or dying. They survive, apparently untouched, apparently indestructible."[12]

It seems evident, by now, that Capp uses the basic devices of the satirist in his narrations. Satire, in itself (by definition, so to speak), has been held to be critical and Capp is obviously and consciously so. He attacks a number of American institutions and values with considerable vehemence, utilizing all the tricks of the satirist's trade.

Let me summarize the main points that I have been trying to make about Capp in this discussion: (1) He uses the standard techniques of the satirist in his dissection of social vices. (2) His use of the grotesque is, ultimately, "an appeal to ideas," as Worcester put it, and is not *just* slapstick and low comedy.[13] Capp is to be distinguished from other comic strip artists who use grotesques by the *degree* of grotesquery and the *large number* of grotesques he employs. These grotesques and caricatures function in a relatively complex manner, as I have continually pointed out. Many of them are symbols and thus contain countless layers of meaning. (3) Capp's continued popularity is due to the quality of his imagination as well as to his choice of subjects that are interesting or "meaningful" to his audience. (I shall point out later that it also is due to his employment of cheese cake.)

Capp is, I would add, to a great degree conscious of what he is doing. He happens to believe, strongly, that it is precisely because characters are "types" that they function in a comic manner. In an article he wrote on "The Comedy of Charlie Chaplin" he said, describing Chaplin's technique: "You will find scores of unique characters, each warmly funny because, no matter how wildly they're drawn, they're based on real, instantly recognizable types."[14]

There is some kind of "recognition" involved in Capp's conception of the comic, which involves an operation of the intellect. Yet essentially Capp's theory of humor is Hobbesian—which sees humor as based upon a feeling of superiority. Hobbes defined laughter as "nothing but the sudden glory arising from sudden conception of some eminence in ourselves; by comparison with the infirmity of others, or with our own formerly."[15] Capp's theory is based on this dictum. And like Hobbes, Capp has a human psychology. He sees man as "full of self-doubt, full of vague feelings of inferiority, full of a desperate need to be reassured."[16]

To assuage these doubts and feelings, Capp presents us with characters who are decidedly inferior and whose ineptness makes us feel fine because it makes us feel superior. For Capp, humor is seen as therapeutic, yet it is based on perversity. As he explains it:

All comedy is based on man's delight in man's inhumanity to man. I know that is so, because I have made forty million people laugh more or less every day for sixteen years, and this has been the basis of all the comedy I have created. I think it is the basis of all comedy.[17]

Interestingly enough, this inhumanity cuts two ways: the aggressors, those who are "inhumane," are seen as depraved—but their victims *also* become depraved and "inhumane," the "ultimate absurdity," as Capp puts it.[18] This conception is, I think, the basis of much of Capp's humor, and explains why we find so much depravity (except for Abner and Mammy) in the stories. This somewhat ironic twist adds a delicious complication to his stories: we do not have a simple case of good versus bad, but have bad versus bad, the depraved fighting the depraved, and a pox on them all. From an ethical standpoint, many of Capp's adventures are quite complex, even though he tends to solve problems by power plays. Mammy is the most powerful person in Dogpatch and its leader; when difficult situations arise, she takes care of them. Capp shows that he is very consistently Hobbesian, in his view of humor and in his use of power as the ultimate way of determining things.

There are two other important points which must be mentioned in discussing Capp's narrative technique: his use of "Fearless Fosdick," the comic strip-within-a-strip, and his satirical fertility rite, the "Sadie Hawkins Day" races.

Fosdick is a satire on the police detective, and, more explicitly, a parody of the famous comic strip character, Dick Tracy. Fosdick, even stupider than Abner, is the latter's favorite comic. He is a member of a city police force and is continually being starved to death, shot, fired, and ill used. He, in turn, abuses his ugly girl friend, Prudence Pimpleton, for he goes with her only because she feeds him.

What is fascinating about this strip-within-a-strip is that we, the readers of "Li'l Abner," are pushed back one step: we read about Abner who reads about Fosdick. Abner is shown to be terribly silly in being so absorbed in this strip, and, by implication, we are told that we are being rather silly in following "Li'l Abner." Capp is able to laugh at us as we laugh at Abner who laughs at Fosdick, and a hierarchy of superiorities is established, with Capp at the top.

By using this device Capp forces us to recognize that "Li'l Abner" *is* a comic strip. Abner is aware that comic strips exist, unlike all the other hundreds and hundreds of comic strip characters who somehow act as if they were real human beings in their own two-dimensional world. By doing this, Capp can exploit the possibilities at hand for being critical because he continually reminds us that, after all, "Li'l Abner" *is* only a comic strip and there is no reason to get offended. He exploits the conventional view that only the solemn can be really serious, and is one of the few comic-strip artists who really is serious.

Most of the others who create humorous comic strips avoid politics and other controversial subjects, which *tends* to be traditional for people functioning in the mass media. As I mentioned before, Capp is able to deal with controversial material by using fantastic characters and by heaping ridicule on almost everything, thus not appearing to be serious. As a result, many people do not take him seriously and he pays a penalty for his freedom. Nevertheless, as will be demonstrated in this study, he still is an effective satirist.

From an anthropological point of view, the most significant aspect of the strip is the annual Sadie Hawkins Day Race, in which the women of Dogpatch have an opportunity to chase unmarried male Dogpatchers and, if they catch one, marry him. Aside from the fact that this is an inversion of the normal situation (the male chasing the female) and therefore somewhat comic, it is interesting for a number of reasons. For one thing, it represents a fertility rite and awakens an awareness of the relationship between the American courtship and more "primitive" rites. In addition, it is an expression, in rather overt terms, of the popular conception (which may be true) that actually, though covertly, the female is more aggressive than the male in seeking out a partner. Third, it has been adopted by quite a number of schools (which have Sadie Hawkins Day Dances) as a legitimate means of allowing girls to escape from their tradition- ally imposed passive roles and show preferences.

What is most fascinating, however, is that comedy has traditionally been associated with fertility rites:

> Comic drama seems related to fertility rituals; it generally celebrates generation, renewal, variety (laughing away any narrow-minded persons who seek to limit life's abundance), and it celebrates man's triumphs over the chances of life.[19]

Capp's continued use of Sadie Hawkins Day was dictated, no doubt, by the reception it received from the public. Curiously enough, for one reason or another, we do have the classically "correct" combination of comedy and the fertility rite, which suggests to me that Capp has some kind of a natural inclination towards what is right, as far as humor is concerned.

Abner was always able to evade "capture" on Sadie Hawkins Day but there was generally a good deal of suspense generated about exactly how he would do so. Until his marriage, the strip was, in a sense, one long courtship—of Abner by Daisy Mae—with interruptions. After the marriage, which was celebrated by the mass media with fanfare including a cover story by *Life* magazine (March 31, 1952), the strip eased into situation comedy episodes, though the fantasy and exaggeration continued and many of Capp's best ideas were to be developed.[20]

Despite the marriage, Abner is still not particularly interested in Daisy Mae, who is Capp's symbol of unrequited love. Capp claims he uses her, and other figures, to reassure people about what he postulates is a perfectly natural condition—a sense of inadequacy and self-doubt. One commentator, Gerhart Saenger, has discussed the relation between Daisy Mae and Abner, and the way love is treated in the strip, in the following manner:

> The prototype of the woman who seeks love but fails to obtain it, is Daisy Mae in the *Li'l Abner* strip. The same strip also supplies the answer to our problems when Abner states: "Love is the most important thing in the world—for other fellows." Love is an important preliminary state in the raising of a large family. Love is dangerous because it leads to marriage, a situation in which, as we have seen [in the comics] men lose their strength. They can preserve their strength only by running away from women, who interfere with their real tasks in life, the seeking and pursuing of adventure.[21]

Saenger's statement about comic strip heroes and their attitude towards women must be qualified, for in some strips the real adventure is the pursuit of love. Nevertheless, in the comic-strip world (and the mass media in general), marriage is *often* accompanied by "negative" results. Love relationships in "Li'l Abner" are most always seen as unsatisfactory: Daisy Mae's love is unrequited because Abner lacks interest, as a result of which their relationship lacks the fundamentals of a decent love affair, two people who care for each other and show it.

Arthur Brodbeck and David Manning White have attributed Abner's lack of interest in Daisy Mae and all attractive young women to his being a "momma's boy":

> Although "Li'l Abner" is concerned with a multitude of facts of American culture, from a Liberace fad to our fantastic needs to "belong" (like the rejected member of the Gourmet Club), there is nonetheless one central problem on which it hinges: *the maternally overprotected boy*, the boy with an overpowering mother.[22]

I would agree that this judgment has a good deal of truth in it, but I think it fails to go deep enough, and that the maternalism is only part of the story. What is also important in the strip—and Brodbeck and White mentioned this without developing it—is the double element of ego and power.

Without power, the ego cannot assert itself; without ego, power will not be utilized. Thus Mammy is the leader of Dogpatch because she is both the most powerful person there and because she feels that she should be the leader. She dominates Abner because she feels that she knows what is best for him. This is the motivation behind her maternalism, I would say. And quite possibly there is a touch of ego in Abner's lack of interest in women: perhaps he is more interested in himself, for he is, like all Cappian characters— an egotist.

To describe the characters in the strip, one would have to say that they are essentially egocentric. Dogpatch (and America) is seen as inhabited by people whose only concern is their own welfare. Their scope is generally limited to matters involving themselves—their wealth, their health, their kin, and nobody has any sense of social obligation. This rugged "individualism" is pushed to ludicrous degrees by Capp, who shows how destructive it can be.

Everyone, except the "fool" Abner, tends to be perverse, and even he has certain questionable qualities.

III

In this chapter I have been especially concerned with formal considerations since I have somewhat arbitrarily decided to deal with a more explicit analysis of Capp's subject interests in the following chapter on dialogue. This does not mean that I have excluded discussions of "subject" but merely that I have not emphasized them. Since this study is informed by the conception that meaning and style are inter-woven, I do not feel that it is possible to separate form and content, though one or the other can be emphasized in any discussion.

I have tried to demonstrate that Capp is an extremely inventive artist in his creation of characters and plots, and that he is a conscious one. The tone of his strip is fundamen-tally ironic and his most characteristic device seems to be the reversal of what is expected. His view of human nature is cynical; we find this both in the strip itself and in his com-ments. Essentially, he is a satirist, and makes use of many of the standard devices of satire in his characterization and plotting, and in his general assessment of society. Further-more, although his medium is the comic strip, there is a decidedly intellectual flavor to his work, as I have pointed out in my discussion of his use of the grotesque.

But what reference does this have for American society and what does it tell us about American values?

This discussion is based upon my assumption that we may, keeping in mind the risks, project from a work to the public that accepts it and come to some guarded conclusions about this public, its values and interests, and so forth. The first and probably the most obvious thing to mention is the form: the comic strip. Its very existence presupposes highly developed (at least from a technical point of view) mass media with a system of syndication and all the other para-phernalia that make printing and distributing a comic strip possible. A comic strip presupposes a certain level of tech-nology and certain kinds of organization for syndication.

Also, to the extent that the comic strip is a romance it is part of a very strong tradition in American literature, and this, in addition to historical matters, possibly explains

White's and Abel's contention that the comic strip is an "American idiom."

Turning to "Li'l Abner," Capp's use of the grotesque can be interpreted as an attack—in purely stylistic terms—on middle-class bourgeois values. There are few middle-class characters in the strip, but everyone's values seem to be rather bourgeois. Most of the characters are either rich and powerful or poor and relatively weak and defenseless. We find rather obvious class conflict—between the rich and the poor—and sectional conflict—between urban and agrarian areas. There is, it seems, a ruling class, a "power-elite," and often the only way this elite is thwarted is by the intervention of Mammy Yokum, a superwoman whose superhuman strength and goodness (and use of magic) are used to achieve social justice.

A recent (December, 1964) episode in the strip demonstrates this extremely well. General Bullmoose, the world's richest man, becomes vexed because, though he has all the money in the world, other people are able to enjoy life—they can eat decently, they can sleep on good mattresses, and so forth. He discovers that the one thing the ordinary man prizes above all other things is a comic strip—"Fearless Fosdick." Bullmoose buys the contract of Fosdick's creator, Lester Gooch, who turns out the strip for Bullmoose's private use. He reads the strip and burns it—so that he can have one pleasure that other people can't. The people threaten rebellion and form vast crowds below Bullmoose's balcony, but he refuses to tell them the contents of the strip. The situation is desperate for all Fosdick lovers, but they are powerless to do anything. Finally they are saved by Mammy, who goes into one of her miraculous spins, finds out what the strip will contain by reading Gooch's mind, and ruins Bullmoose's plan. He capitulates, saying that he is unable to contend with the infinite goodness of Mammy Yokum. As he puts it, freeing Gooch: "GO, Gootch!! I've learned there's ONE power GREATER than money—the iron will of a GOOD WOMAN."[23]

It took a miracle to save the people from Bullmoose and his power, and sometimes in the strip no miracles happen. The rich, unscrupulous businessmen are successful. If we project Capp's view to American society, we find a rather pessimistic assessment made of our democracy, and its egalitarian pretensions. It might be argued that this episode shows how egalitarian American society is, but this reading does not take into account the ending. The people were "saved" by a miracle, and relying on miracles is not a positive way of ensuring democracy.

The grotesque implies a norm and an examination of its subject, which means that the readers of the strip—except for children—are forced continually to make evaluations. Since "Li'l Abner" is full of socially relevant subjects, it means that at least on a very simple level, and perhaps in a somewhat unconscious manner, American society and values are continually being held up for scrutiny.

It may be agreed that generally speaking the comic strip is "simple" and its world a simple one, or perhaps an oversimplified one. The vast popularity of the comics might then be explained in several ways: the American public is looking for relief—some kind of certainty, some "fixities" in a world which presents them with complexity and with problems that seem insoluble. Or, the public is seeking to escape from the real world into some kind of a fantasy world, some vast, collective "daydream" from which they need not emerge. The only thing wrong with the second interpretation is that even in the comics we find conflicts and problems, so that the escape offered from troubles is of negligible value.

Also, I should argue that the supposed simplicity is, itself, an oversimplification, as we see in Capp's "Li'l Abner."

The readers want problems which they can grasp, and relatively reasonable solutions. In "Li'l Abner" the solutions are telescoped, as is all the action, and are very abrupt. A reader can grasp them easily and feel some kind of satisfaction when he sees the triumph of goodness and morality over evil and selfishness. I shall argue in the conclusion of this study that people read "Li'l Abner"—and other comic strips —to learn about life, and not to escape from it. But before I do this, it is necessary to offer a more adequately developed analysis of the range of Capp's interests and the specific objects of his satire. I have attempted this in the following chapter on his dialogue.

CHAPTER 4

Dialogue and Damnation in Li'l Abner

I

As a corollary to my conception of form, in itself, as having a kind of meaning, I assume that Capp's desire to satirize American society has greatly affected his style. We see this especially well in his use of grotesques, caricatures, stereotypes, and fools. I have already alluded to this subject in my analysis of Capp's narratives, but I would like to explore it even further in this discussion of his dialogue[1] and, more specifically, his use of language. The very form that Capp's narratives assume has implicitly a socially critical "content." In his use of language, however, Capp has been able to be much more explicit.

There is something questionable about separating dialogue from art work in discussing comic strips—for the two form a unity in this "impure" form—but I have done this so that I can look at each of these aspects more carefully.

This discussion of Capp's dialogue should be useful in helping to characterize his style—focusing attention on that which is personal, individual, or unique in "Li'l Abner." In analyzing some of Capp's major subject interests I shall discuss the particular devices Capp uses in his dialogue. I shall also offer some suggestions about what the strip—and especially his dialogue—reveals about American society.

The most obvious fact about the dialogue in "Li'l Abner" is the amount of it. Capp uses a great deal more dialogue than many other comic strip writers. A look at the "zoot-suit" adventure reproduced in the last chapter shows this. There are numerous large balloons full of dialogue, and Capp has also reproduced newspapers and newspaper copy. In fact, the first third of the adventure has almost no action; it just shows people sitting around tables carrying on conversations. It is the absurd nature of the situations and the conversations that keeps us interested. A second third of the episode is devoted to clips from newspapers and more conferences, and a bare third is devoted to Abner's actual adventures as "Zoot-Suit Yokum." This story is a bit unusual; generally there is much more action, but it does point out how important the dialogue can be in "Li'l Abner." There is so much dialogue in "Li'l Abner"—in the form of balloons, clips, etc.—that one almost gets the idea that Capp's major interest is the continuity and the language. (Actually, they are probably what is most Cappian about the strip. Like most comic strip originators, Capp has assistants who do all the drudge labor. He writes the continuities, originates the characters, and does some finishing work on the faces. The assistants do the rest.[2])

II

Capp's dialogue can be characterized as using the following basic devices: exaggeration, playfulness, paradox, and parody. The exaggerations, which are evident in the drawings and plots as well as the dialogues, are probably most typical of the Cappian technique. There is hardly an aspect of the strip that is not exaggerated, from the vernacular dialects to the punctuation. This rather obvious exaggeration is Capp's way of disarming us—so that we can't get angry about his social criticisms, and this poses a problem for him: to the extent that we *are* disarmed by him we dismiss his criticism. This means he pays a price for his exaggeration, but quite evidently he thinks it is worth what it costs, for he is able to range very widely precisely because he does not seem to be "serious."

Even Capp's punctuation is highly exaggerated. Almost every sentence ends with two exclamation marks, which suggests that the characters are doing the equivalent of shouting at each other. The exclamation marks are really quite symbolic of the makeup of the strip and its characters; many of whom tend to be, or think they are, laws unto themselves, so that what each says is uniquely important. Ultimately, of course, the device is self-defeating, for if everything is important then nothing is uniquely important.

Capp also uses a large number of exclamatory grunts and groans such as "gasp!!" and "sob!!" which are evidences of an extremely subjective approach to reality and which imply on the part of the characters that there are aspects of reality which conventional language cannot do justice to.

Suzanne Langer suggests this in her discussion of exclamations:

> But the symbolic presentation of subjective reality for contemplation is not only tentatively beyond the reach of language—that is not merely beyond the words we have; it is impossible in the essential frame of language. That is why those semanticists who recognize only discourse as a symbolic form must regard the whole life of feeling as formless, chaotic, capable only of symptomatic expression, typified in exclamations like "Ah!" "Ouch!" "My sainted aunt!"[3]

These exclamatory utterances are used by Capp to show how unsophisticated and uncouth the characters are—they are amazed by everything and rendered speechless, so they can only respond with gasps and groans. But beyond any particular situation, we find what probably is an intuitive conception, on Capp's part, of the way the emotional lives of his characters can be presented. It seems to be similar to what Langer talks about in reference to feelings—or the presentation of subjective reality—as beyond the reach of language. Capp's exclamations may be a relatively simplistic solution to this problem, but he does not have much language at his disposal; for one thing, he is a comic strip artist and there are certain technical limitations in the form. (Also, he can show expression and feeling in his drawings of faces, so he has a tool that is 'beyond language" and denied those who are restricted to it.)

The gasps represent the emotional responses of the characters to situations, and function so as to let the reader know what he should feel in any given situation. When Mammy utters a "Gasp!!" upon seeing the square-eyed people, we understand that we are to feel surprised; and when a lawyer tells Abner "You'd better see your (shudder!!)

hinheritance before you haul it away, you pitiful hunfortunate," we know that Abner is in for some traumatic experience. Thus, the exclamations are stage directions of a sort, that tell us how to react to any given situation.

It is no accident then that the most recent collection of "Li'l Abner" stories was subtitled "The GASP!! World of Li'l Abner," for it is a world of extremes, of strong emotional outbreaks that can only be presented as exclamatory utterances. Capp also uses heavy face print and large print for emphasis. This is a convention of the medium, but Capp makes use of it more than the average comic strip artist does. In fact, almost every balloon has boldface print or enlarged print, which means that by using a relatively mechanical device, Capp forces the reader to make distinctions continually. There is no relaxing, so to speak, for words and phrases keep jumping out of the page at us. The size of the print tells us the loudness of the language, so that Capp is able to create a vocal range to parallel emotional intensity. All this is artificial and somewhat mechanical, yet it is in keeping with the personalities of the characters. In a gasp world full of naive types, every other event *is* a crisis. The characters are all very excitable and we can expect the emphasis that we find in their speech.

In addition to the mechanical or typographical means that Capp utilizes, we find exaggeration in the language of his characters (as well as in the drawings of them, which I shall discuss in the next chapter). We find a remarkable consistency that ranges through the conception of the characters, their speech, and the way it is reproduced.

The following selection, taken from a Cappian satirization of gourmandism, demonstrates this. The characters are all fantastic; they push gourmandism to rather absurd conclusions; and their language is in keeping with all the madness. Bounder J. Roundheels, a fat little man, has been trying to join the "Gourmets' Club" since 1909 and has been rejected by P. Fangsgood Droolsby, head of the club, nine times, for not having food that is "unusual" enough. The following conversation takes place after Roundheels' last rejection:

ROUNDHEELS: Life isn't worth LIVING unless I can get into the "Gourmets' Club"!! It's the world's most exclusive organization of lovers of unique food.

A vacancy occurred in 1909——when a member STARVED to death because there was nothing left in the world good enough for him to eat!!

ABNER: Tsk!! Tsk!! Hard t' PLEASE, huh?

NINE times yo' has tried t'git into th' "GOOR-MAYS' CLUB." Nine times yo' has FLOPPED—Huh, Roundheels? Yo' got ONE mo' chance, huh? Yo' gotta REALLY whip up somethin' unusual THIS time—huh, Roundheels?

ROUNDHEELS: YES, just ONE!! Ah yes!! They LAUGHED at my "heart of ripened century plant salad!!" They coldly BURPED at my "jellied armadillo brains with unborn mushrooms"!! They ordered me off the premises when I submitted my "gnats' kidneys on the half shell"!! *Sigh!!* There's just ONE thing left!!

ABNER: A good dose o' Bi-carby-by-nate o' soda—huh, Roundheels?

ROUNDHEELS: NO, lad!! the RAREST DISH OF ALL

> "—ROAST RUMP OF TREE-DWELL-
> ING ELEPHANT WITH ECSTASY
> SAUCE." Gathering the materials for that
> dish may cost ALL my millions and
> heaven KNOWS how many LIVES!!

ABNER: Hard t' git, huh?[4]

In this conversation, we find Abner acting as a goad, leading Roundheels on, to reveal the patent absurdity of his passionate desire to "belong,"—or, more precisely, his mono-mania. The difference in dialects is worth noticing. Round-heels speaks normal English, but the contrast between the language he speaks and the things he talks about is comic. Abner speaks his typical vernacular, which is humorous, yet he seems much more rational. In this case, Abner is function-ing as an *eiron*, or dissembler (though he is, more specifi-cally, what Frye calls *homoloichos*, a buffoon, and the *agroikos*, rustic, variety of this species). He is playing the *eiron* to Roundheels' *alazon*, or boaster.[5]

Despite the differences between the two characters, they are fundamentally alike. They are both compulsive, uncom-promising egotists, though Roundheels is active and forceful, and Abner is passive and carried along by events. Both are so uncompromising, that they cannot but act *destructively*. In this story, Roundheels, unable to obtain a rare ingredient for his concoction, has himself boiled down into a drop for the ecstasy sauce. Droolsby eats the dinner (thereby unknow-ingly committing cannibalism) and accepts him into the club, but it is too late.

DROOLSBY: AHH! That "ecstasy sauce" was out of this
world!! As president and grand exalted
taster of the Gourmets' club, I APPROVE
of candidate Roundheels' dish!! BRING IN
THE GENIUS!!

COOK: Alas, M'sieu Droolsby—I (sob!) HAVE!!

DROOLSBY: I don't see him!!

COOK: Naturally!! HE (sob) was ze "ecstasy sauce"!!

DROOLSBY: Y-you mean that Roundheels HIMSELF . . .??

COOK: Yes, M'sieu!! Y-YES! Sob!!

DROOLSBY: Egad! He WAS a man of good taste! (Smack!) I will award him a posthumous membership in the Gourmets' club. He DE-SERVES it! He gave ALL!![6]

We do not feel very sorry for Roundheels, for in another part of the episode he is revealed to be a monster, willing to destroy the Yokums to get their pig for his ecstasy sauce; still, the important thing is that he was also willing to destroy himself to satisfy his ego and get into the Gourmets' Club. (This particular situation exemplifies what seems to be some kind of an oral fixation on the part of Capp's characters. Food plays a tremendous part in their lives, often to the exclusion of other drives such as sex.)

The same type of thing happens to Abner: he marries Daisy Mae *only* because he has pledged to do whatever Fosdick does. After Fosdick marries, Abner marries Daisy Mae. Ultimately he learns that Fosdick's marriage only took place in a dream, but it is too late for Abner, for as Mammy explains:

But, son—try to unnerstan'. YORE marriage warn't no dream!!—It don't matter no more—whut FOSDICK done done—or whut Fosdick didn't done done—YO' IS MARRIED—HOPELESSLY—PERMANENTLY—MARRIED!![7]

In these cases each character is willing to sacrifice what is most important to himself—his life or his "freedom"—to satisfy his ego. Roundheels gets into the Gourmets' Club, but dies to do it; Abner keeps his word, he keeps his pledge to the Fearless Fosdick Fan Club and get married, but at the cost of his "freedom." They pay an exorbitant price to prove that they are worthy, either of membership or trust. Capp is exposing the absurdity of uncompromising and uncritical devotion to causes by showing to what ridiculous *consequences* it can lead.

The excesses and absurdities involved in the Roundheels story suggest some kind of kinship with the tall tale of the West, except that here the tale is dramatized rather than told. Instead of having several characters trying to outdo each other in concocting fantastic meals, Roundheels keeps on outdoing himself. But the controlling conception of the tall tale, the heaping on of exaggerations, is adhered to. We see also several devices of linguistic humor: the juxtaposition of dialect and conventional language, the use of "queer cataloguing," obvious exaggeration, and a rather horrible pun.

The pun is probably Capp's favorite form of playing around with language—and he does play with language a great deal. The pun is conventionally held to be the "lowest form" of humor in that it makes the least demands upon our intelligence. However, as D. H. Munro put it in *Argument of Laughter*, discussing wit and puns:

> We laugh at plays upon words even when they are not accompanied by satire. . . . The joke, it may be said, lies wholly in tracing a connection between two dissimilar things: the implication may or may not be present that the two are after all really similar.

> But this is not the whole story. For if the connection turns out to be purely verbal, we feel dissatisfied with

the joke. The pun *qua* pun is the weakest form of wit. Plays upon words are felt to be merely puerile unless they are accompanied by some play upon meaning.[8]

The point that must be made is this: if the pun is merely a play on words, it tells us nothing and is just an example of simpleminded playfulness. If, however, the pun is related to the situation and does have something to do with the meaning, then it has validity and is an example of wit.

Many of Capp's puns are genuinely witty[9] and some of them are ingenious. Others are unimaginative and second rate. In the zoot-suit satire the zoot-suiters take the slogan "A zoot-suit on every man or bust." The pun here is rather obvious: the term "bust" means either "the breasts of a woman" or "burst" (as in "California or bust"). Another example—on one of Capp's favorite subjects, pork—displays a lack of real inventiveness:

A page from "Who's Who in American Pork"
FATBACK, J. ROARINGHAM

Born 1900—Porkland, Oregon. Showed early talent for swinery. After modest start, hit the pig-time by combining Central Pork with Yellowstone National Pork. In 1927, bought out Hyde Pork, Inc. Changed name of exclusive New York street to "Pork Avenue," and erected 250-story Hampire State Building.[10]

Although this passage has a number of playful aspects, its puns are not particularly imaginative: Capp substitutes pork for park four times, switches big-time to pig-time and Empire to Hampire. The basic idea of substituting pork for park is not terribly ingenious and the repetition does not add to the humor.

On the other hand, Capp's playfulness with the Shmoo is quite interesting and rather complicated, due in a large degree to his employment of paradox. The Shmoo has been described as:

> . . . a small white squash with two tiny legs, a pair of eyes and wispy mustache hairs. Nothing else. It was a rather amorphous object. . . . The Shmoo laid eggs (Grade A), gave milk (Grade A), and died of sheer ecstasy if you looked at it with hunger in your eyes. The Shmoo loved to be eaten because food makes people happy. Anything that makes people happy makes a Shmoo happy. Fry a Shmoo and it comes out chicken. Broil it and it comes out steak. Shmoo eyes make splendid suspender buttons. Shmoo hide cut thin is fine leather; cut thick, it is the best lumber. Shmoo whiskers make magnificent toothpicks. The Shmoo, in a word, takes care of all the world's wants, and we can never run out of Shmoon.[11]

The Shmoo is shown to disrupt the entire status quo, to throw society into pandemonium, so that ultimately a massive campaign is launched to exterminate them. The motto of the campaign is "Kill Shmoos—Shmoos are BAD because they're so GOOD!!"[12]

There is more to this than just the paradox of something being bad because it is good. The word "Shmoo" is quite probably a modification of the Jewish term *Schmo* or *Schmuck*, which means either "fool" ("booby," "nitwit") or "penis."[13] It also carries with it the suggestion of somebody "bad"—(it is not good to be a fool) so that when Capp says Shmoos are bad, literally speaking, he is telling the truth. Thus the Shmoo is bad "by definition," and because it is so good that it shakes the foundations of society, which is seen to be based on selfishness and exploitation:

> The reason Shmoos is th' worst thing that kin happen to hoomanity—is wif Shmoos around, nobody has to fight

nobody else—nor cheat nobody else, nor work thar hearts out fo' nobody else!!—An wifout THEM sports —th' whole world would come to a stop!!![14]

People have seen the Shmoo as Christ—complete goodness which society cannot accept and hence destroys, but I think that this view is unjustifiable. It is based upon only one particular quality of the Shmoo and fails to account for others. The reason people have seen the Shmoo as Christ is, I think, because they have sensed that the tale is a parable—that is, it is rich in symbolic meaning and it has an obvious moral, with which Capp ends *The Life and Times of the Shmoo*:

> Folks don't need these LI'L Shmoos!!—They already GOT one—th' biggest Shmoo of all—TH' EARTH, ITSELF!! Jest like these li'l Shmoos, IT'S ready t'give ev'rybody ev'rything they need!! Ef only folks stopped a-fightin', an' a-grabbin'—they'd realize that THIS Shmoo—th' earth—got plenty o' ev'rything—fo' ev'rybody!!![15]

Capp is saying that we don't need little Shmoos—to take care of our wants—because the earth itself can do so, if we don't abuse it, and ourselves.

The most intriguing thing about the Shmoo, as I see it, is that it is a phallic symbol,[16] and I say this for a number of reasons. The drawing of the Shmoo looks somewhat like an erect penis coming from a gigantic scrotum which emerges from between two legs. (We might think of it as a wildly reductionistic fantastic creature—man reduced to a penis.) Capp also says that "they multiplies wifout th' slightest encouragement,"[17] which brings to mind the reproductive function of the penis.   Then there is the Yiddish meaning of the term *"schmuck,"* which is "penis" or "fool." But even the English term "fool" would almost be enough to support this view, for it comes from the Latin *follis,* which means bellows, bag, or sac. The bladder is one of the standard "tools" of the fool and is associated with low comedy. There is a curious confluence of meanings here which, I believe, supports my interpretation. What I am suggesting then is that the Shmoo *can* be taken to symbolize *masculine sexuality,* unrestricted and uninhibited by society. Since society, as it is presently organized, cannot tolerate this, the Shmoo must be destroyed—for *it* will not tolerate anything less. We have a conflict that reduces itself to absolutes—free love or castration—and castration wins.

This means that the destruction of the Shmoos is an extremely complicated matter. Politically it is a condemnation of society, which is built upon such a foul combination of excessive and destructive individualism, exploitation, and dishonesty that it cannot tolerate love and goodness. Psychologically it suggests some kind of a castration complex in the American male. He must repress any dream he might have of an uninhibited or free sexuality and return to a "normal" way of life.

The different ways in which the Shmoos are killed are interesting. In the first book, *The Life and Times of the Shmoo,* the Shmoos are killed by being shot—the symbol of life is overpowered by a symbol of death, and death in the form of firing squads (Shmooicide squads), which suggests that this is some kind of official ceremony. In the *Return of the Shmoo* they are killed by being exposed to a picture of Pappy, the weak father. Mammy, however, was the one responsible for this idea. She "saves" the nation—that is, she is responsible for the mass castration and thereby insures that she will retain her power.

Generally speaking, the Shmoos have been interpreted as having only economic implications and Capp has discussed this matter in some detail in a recent *New Yorker* interview:

> "What's different this time is the mail," the cartoonist continued, pointing his cigarette towards an enormous stack of letters on a silver tray. "Formerly, all the McCarthyites were down on me. Shmoos were Socialistic, they said. Shmoos were a blatant and treacherous attack on capitalism. *Now*, those same guys are writing 'Atta boy Al! We see you're right in there pitching for us.' This is all beyond me, but it may have some crazy connection with the fact that I've used the *new* shmoos as a kind of protest against this insane business of foreign aid we're in—this nonsense of give, give, give, with no strings attached."[18]

Here we see a pretty obvious example of Capp's social commitment: he believes that politics is his realm and that he should comment upon it, using, of course, the humor of his strip to do so from a somewhat "privileged" position. We see this even more as the interview continues and he talks about how he came to create the Shmoo:

> The truth is there's no particular economic theory behind the shmoo. I made it—well, from the kind of sheer desperation that seems to lead me into everything I do. I had set out to find the great, unrealizable dream of the people and then to realize that dream for them in the strip. What would happen, I wanted to know, if there were shmoos around—that is, if there were no more cause for confusion, work, war, crime, and so on in the world? If there were nothing but plenty, nothing but pleasure, nothing but love? Well, my own sense of horror dictated the rest. Shmoos, of course, would have to be destroyed. Society would prove itself too organized to and around pain to exist without it [*sic*]. *That* was horrifyingly clear.[19]

All of this is, of course, evident in the episodes dealing with the Shmoos. In a sense, the confrontation of the Shmoo, a symbol of absolute love and goodness, and the world with all its imperfections and such, was bound to lead to the destruction of these animals. It was an impossible situation, even in dreamland, for a society with *nothing* but plenty, love, and pleasure is quite probably psychologically, physiologically, and politically impossible.

It is difficult to describe the Shmoo adequately, or to explain how it affected people, but something about it—possibly a combination of all the things I've talked about—must have come through. More than seven hundred thousand people bought copies of *The Life and Times of the Shmoo* and more than seventy-five items such as cottage cheese in Shmoo jars, Shmoo balloons, and such were sold at the height of the fad's popularity.

III

I would like to make a distinction between the devices Capp uses to create what Walter Blair calls "humor of phraseology"[20]—such as exaggeration, word-play and paradox—and Capp's interests—that is, those aspects of language that fascinate him and which he sometimes repeats in "Li'l Abner." There are three essential "qualities" of language that seem to intrigue him: (1) the effect that language can have on men's actions; (2) the nature or process of definition; and (3) the relation that exists between names and things.

We can see one instance of Capp's fascination with the power of language in his creation of the expert, J. Colossal McGenius, the great "idea man" whose advice costs ten thousand dollars a word but "is worth it." McGenius is used for humorous purposes. He tells long jokes, which at ten thousand dollars a word cost his clients a fortune, and often burps and belches, at ten thousand dollars a burp. But Mc-Genius is "worth it" because he understands human nature and knows what motivates people; his services are necessary, no matter what the price. Capp's putting a tag of ten thousand dollars a word (or sound) on his advice serves only to emphasize, by ridicule, the importance we tend to place upon expertism, upon idea men. McGenius offers his services to whoever can pay his price; in this story he both creates the zoot-suit mania and destroys it, so that the $1,760,000 it cost the zoot-suit makers for his advice was misspent. He is shown to be capable of doing as much harm as good.

Another aspect of language that intrigues Capp is the matter of definition. He is fond of the dialectical process and uses it upon occasion. There is one episode I have already mentioned in which he explores what we might call "the nature of man." Tiny Yokum and Fatback (his boss) have climbed to the top of Mt. Neverbin and have discovered "Abominable Snow-hams," which smell like the finest roast ham.[21] Fatback has been granted exclusive rights to develop Mt. Neverbin "and all its wild life" as the result of some political chicanery done by his lackey, Senator Phogbound. The following conversation takes place between Fatback and Tiny Yokum:[22]

FATBACK: If these abominable snow-hams TASTE as good as they SMELL and FEEL—I'LL MAKE BILLIONS!! Get that portable stove going!!

TINY: Yassuh!!

FATBACK: We'll roast a LI'L one!!

TINY: But, is yo' shore it haint a li'l PERSON, suh?

Dialogue

FATBACK: Open your mouth Sonny—JUST a li'l wider!! AHA!!—it's IN!!—Now, we'll roast you to a fine golden brown!! (He puts an apple in the Snow-ham's mouth.)

TINY: NOPE!! Not till we is shore they haint PEOPLE!!

FATBACK: ?? What makes you think they ARE?

TINY: Wal—they builds HOMES like people—

FATBACK: BEAVERS build homes!!

TINY: Th' mammys carries th' young ones around!!

FATBACK: KANGAROOS carry THEIR young!!

TINY: But—they MIGHT be people!! LOOK!!— They're skeered o' bein broiled!!

FATBACK: So are LOBSTERS!

TINY: They LOVES each other like people!!

FATBACK: RABBITS love each other—MORE than people!!

It should be noted that this last phrase is a pun on "love." Capp is referring to the sexual fecundity of the rabbit as well as to his sense of affection.

They settle upon an arbitrator, Senator Phogbound, who tests the Snow-hams to see whether or not they are human beings. He gives them a sample ballot with his name and his opponent's name on it and asks them to mark one. They all mark the name of the opponent, so Phogbound, realizing that they could vote him out of office if human, declares that they are animals.

Fatback starts shipping them off to the slaughterhouse, but one of the trucks slips into reverse. Just as Fatback is about to be run over, a Snow-ham saves him.

121

TINY: One of them manly li'l critters SAVED YORE LIFE!! Don't THET prove he's HOOMIN?

FATBACK: It proves he's a FOOL!!—ON TO THE SLAUGHTER HOUSE!!

Tiny sees the Snow-hams kissing each other before they arrive at the slaughterhouse and concludes they are humans. He stops the trucks and lets them free.

TINY: Ah is gonna SAVE mah li'l fella-citizens!!

FATBACK: YOU'RE NOT SAVING ANY OF YOUR FELLOW-CITIZENS. YOU'RE STEAL-ING MY MEAT!!

Eventually the case is brought to court. Fatback's case is handled by J. Rumbleton Bagpipe, an internationally cele-brated lawyer; the Snow-hams are represented by Apassionata Fiasco, an "exchange graduate law student from Mexico who is seeking experience." Bagpipe bases his case on two things which are posited to be uniquely human: willingness to take advantage of people and laughing at others' misfortune. He places a man and a Snow-ham together on the witness stand and asks:

BAGPIPE: If you had something I needed DESPER-ATELY, would you charge me TEN times the regular price?

MAN: YOU BET!! I'M no fool!

The Snow-ham shakes its head "no," which, says Bagpipe, is a "TOTALLY SENSELESS UNHUMAN REACTION." Bagpipe then purposely slips on a banana peel and everyone except the Snow-ham laughs.

Dialogue

BAGPIPE: Every human being in the court LAUGHED
when I nearly fractured my skull—But—
this miserable Snow-ham rushed to HELP
me!!—That proves it has no human sense
of humor!! It's just an ANIMAL!! I rest my
case.

The Snow-hams are saved because it turns out, ultimately, that the judge is related to the Snow-hams. His father
was one of the few Snow-hams who "left home and made
good." Immediately, the judge (who had been planning on
eating a Snow-ham for dinner) finds them "human" and dis-
misses the case.

Capp's exaggeration serves both to mask the brutality
and horror of the story (which once again involves cannibalism), and to ridicule and bring into question the ethics and
fundamental decency of human beings and a number of
social institutions: business, politics, and the law. Ultimately,
self interest is seen as the guide to conduct. Fatback was willing to slaughter human beings and feed them to others
because he would realize a profit on the transaction. Fatback
knows the Snow-hams are human. We see this when he says
"Open your mouth *Sonny*" (emphasis added). Yet his impulse to make a profit overrides his very humanity.

The interesting thing to note here is that aside from
the cynicism behind the absurd characters and situations, we
have a methodical investigation into what being human
means. There is a dialogue carried on in which various suggestions offered by Tiny as to what is human are shown to
apply to animals. Then, the Snow-hams are put to three
different *tests*, which involve comparing them with human
beings. In every case, they are shown to be better than human
beings, at least, the kind of human beings Capp peoples his
strip with. The Snow-hams are kind, gentle, honest, sym-

123

pathetic, and fair, and the human beings who are judging them suffer by comparison.

The method is experiential, and though the characters in the episode (other than Tiny and the Snow-hams) are demonic, they are pragmatic demons, who test things, carry on experiments, and so forth. Capp defines things by giving examples, not by having recourse to absolutes or essences. The Shmoos are "defined" according to what they do: lay Grade A eggs, give Grade A milk, and so forth. We also saw this in the story about the square-eyed people. Mammy comes across a square-eyed little boy caught in a wolf trap, and the following thoughts occur to her in the course of the story:

She takes him out and reflects: (—"This chile!!—it got square eyes—but it yowls like any OTHER chile!!")

She notices him bleeding: ("An' th' pore li'l thing bleeds like any other chile—")

She sees that his mother is excited: ("An his MAMMY!!—SHE'S just as shocked as a ROUND-eyed mammy!!—")
(—"Th' tears she's a-cryin'—they's like ALL mammys' tears, irregardless o' color or shape of eyes!!—")

As a result of all this observation and reflective thought she comes to the *conclusion* that the square-eyed people are just like other people, except that their eyes are different. As she puts it: "Th' li'l DIFF'RENCES between folks shouldn't hide th' big things thass th' SAME 'bout all of us!!"[23] The recourse to exemplification suggests that ther are no really adequate "limiting" definitions, and Capp shows this in a parody he made of Charles Schulz's *Happiness is a Warm Puppy*. Capp uses his typical device of inversion and irony in such examples of happiness as:

> Happiness is being bothered (girl being whistled at).
> Happiness is not being bothered (cars on lovers' lane).
> Happiness is not getting caught (crook escaping police).
> Happiness is getting caught (girl under mistletoe).[24]

Everything is seen as related to context, or to put it another way, to the particular situation. Capp is imitating Schulz here. Both, however, are writing within the conventions of the medium, for the comic strip is based upon things being spelled out explicitly.

The third major quality of language that seems to fascinate Capp is the relation between words and things, and more specifically between names and things. Capp creates fantastic names for his incredible characters, in much the same way as the ancient Greeks and Romans, the Restoration wits, and so many others did. Dumpington Van Lump is, as his name suggests, a rich lump and J. Colossal McGenius is a genius, both as aptly named as Aristophanes' heroine Lysistrata, which means "She who disbands the armies."[25]

It is generally held that the function of a name is to distinguish a person, to give him some kind of individuality and a way of identifying himself so that he can have a subjective existence. If this is true, then we find that Capp is playing down the individuality of his characters and emphasizing their symbolic natures and roles. This interpretation emphasizes the moral nature of the strip and suggests its kinship with the medieval morality play. The morality play has been defined in *The Reader's Companion To World Literature* as:

> a type of medieval drama in which the characters are personified abstractions: Everyman, Good Deeds, Faith, Mercy, Anger, etc. The morality play is a fusion of two streams—medieval allegory as in the *Romance of the Rose,* and the religious drama of the mystery plays.

. . . The two main themes of the religious morali-
ties are the struggle between good and evil powers for
man's soul, and the journey or pilgrimage of life, with
its choice of eternal destinations. Vices, devils, etc. gave
a considerable opportunity for low comedy, and the far-
cical element was especially developed in France.
Though the morality was essentially religious, it was
also used to inculcate ethical or educational ideals and
to provide thinly disguised political commentary or
satire.[26]

The title of the strip, "Li'l Abner," is ironic, for we
see that Abner is a towering giant of a man, with bulging
biceps and heroic proportions. At the same time the title
is correct, because we find that Abner's mind is undeveloped
and he has little brainpower. The choice of the name Abner
is meaningful. For one thing, Abner suggests a rural type, a
"hick" or a "hillbilly," and thus some kind of a fool. Also,
there is an association of the name Abner with something
foolish in the Bible:

Died Abner as a fool dieth?
Thy hands were not bound,
Nor thy feet put into fetters:
As a man falleth before wicked men,
So falleth thou.[27]

In the Bible reference was made to Abner's death at the
hands of Joab, which cannot be connected with the strip.
However, if we interpret the term "falleth" figuratively, so
as to mean being the dupe or victim, then it is startlingly relevant. Also, Abner is Hebrew for "light bringer," so he might
be legitimately seen as an exposer of folly and human
stupidity.

Abner's father is called Pappy and is shown to be a
bungling, weak person. Strangely enough, both his *name* and

his *role* go back at least as far as Roman comedy. In his notes to Petronius' *Satyricon*, William Arrowsmith, the translator, discusses an early form of the comedy called the Atellan farce, and says: "Normally, an Atellan farce had four stock characters: the stupid father (Pappus), the clown (Bucco), the fool (Maccus), and the wise man (Dossennus)."[28] This is just a coincidence I imagine, that stems from the hillbilly word for father being "pappy." Once again, his name is his role, and the same applies to his wife, Mammy.

Anyone who wishes to stress the oedipal nature of Abner's relationship with his mother may take some comfort in the conjecture that in addition to naming her role, "Mammy" may be a perversion of "Mamie," which some see as a diminution of the French *m'amie,* (my lady friend), or *m'aimee* (my beloved).[29] If one were to push this hypothesis further, we would find why Abner has no interest in girls: he is not just a momma's boy, but has a severe Oedipus complex.

Daisy Mae is a beautiful flower waiting to be plucked by Abner. Physically she is the "dream girl" of the American sexual fantasy. Abner's total lack of interest in her seems ludicrous and perverse, for though the conventions of the comic strip tend to prohibit marriage between characters, they do not prohibit love affairs. Abner doesn't touch Daisy, even though he "may."

Fearless Fosdick is also another "rarity" in that he is a burlesque of the famous comic strip character Dick Tracy. His name is meant to suggest the "Dick" in Dick Tracy and also to tell us his profession, since the slang term for detective also happens to be "dick."[30] I have already mentioned how Capp uses this device to create the unusual situation of having a comic strip character read the comics. Thus, when Capp ridicules the comic strip reader of comics, he is *really* ridiculing the actual comic strip reader and popular culture.

In addition to these main characters, there are hundreds of others, among them Available Jones, Quentin Rasputin-reynolds, Mandrake P. Mothball, the Scragg Brothers, Rockwell P. Squeezeblood, and so on. Capp's ability to create weird characters with strange names has been likened to Dickens' and with some justification, I believe.

Finally, the strip is given topical interest by numerous allusions to famous people and incidents, all of which are intended to amuse the readers. This device is typical of comedy—there are many kinds of topical allusions in the work of Aristophanes, the great Greek comedian, and in the works of other comedians since his day. The topical allusions in "Li'l Abner," and other humorous works, are interesting because they tell us something about the audience's frame of reference, but they also serve to "date" the work, so that it loses some of its meaning for later readers. This, no doubt, is of little concern to Capp.

IV

In this discussion of Capp's dialogue—his use of strange names, puns, paradoxes, grunts, and so forth—I have tried to demonstrate that there is a fusion of subject and style that has produced a satirical work which is both artistically satisfying and socially relevant. Above the level of action, there is rather obvious political comment, which is presented in the form of disquisitions and by characters that are caricatures and grotesques. Capp attacks "rugged individualism" by presenting a rugged individualist whose distorted personality mirrors his distorted picture of the world and his place in it. We see how destructive the "rugged individualist" can be when he is given free reign to pursue his aims to their logical, but absurd (in the sense of being anti-social and stupid), conclusions.

All of this suggests a definite kinship between "Li'l Abner" and the morality play: the political and social comment, the satire, the type characterization, the ethical purpose—are all modernized, but nonetheless are similar in form to topical features of the ancient morality play. We even find that there is generally a symbolic significance to the names, though Capp often uses these names for purposes of ridicule. But Capp's society is not as ordered as that in the Middle Ages and there is a good deal of confusion.

The chaos of the strip is, perhaps, a reflection of what is to Capp a chaotic society. He is extremely cynical about people's goodness—everyone is motivated by self-interest and the desire for personal gain. In "Li'l Abner" we find what might be called "the death of the heroic." Almost everyone is selfish and unscrupulous, and Abner, the hero of the strip, is a fool—or, perhaps, an anti-hero. In the episode in which Abner was "Zoot-Suit Yokum" and a hero, he was the dupe of men who were making millions. And, to qualify for this position, he had to be the stupidest person in the country. There is little room for heroism in the strip—or at least for conscious heroism—and this combination of cynicism and the non-heroic reflects, I think, a strong sense of alienation on Capp's part. Being a cynic he would quite naturally find it impossible to believe in heroism, and in this position we are left, so to speak, at the mercy of chance.

The improvisation that we find in the conclusions of many of the episodes—the use of magic, the strange coincidences (that the Judge was a Snow-Ham), the accidents—mean two things then. The first is that Capp often finds it difficult to come up with a conclusion that is logical, satisfying, and compressed enough to be suitable; the second, that they reflect his view of society. The "world" of "Li'l Abner" may be in some respects a simple one, but the problems Abner becomes involved in are not as simple as they seem.

I think we find this in the language itself. Capp's use of an American vernacular is, in itself, an "affront" to the social order, and has strong egalitarian implications. But in addition, his use of puns and plays of language show an awareness of complexity. The paradoxes and ambiguities suggest, on the linguistic level, a complex picture of society and social problems. The double meanings in words imply that perhaps there are double "solutions" to problems—that we cannot allow ourselves oversimplifications either in formulating or solving them. Capp's presentation of insane formalists and grotesques shows us what terrible things can happen when we do oversimplify, when we allow our "quest for certainty" to overwhelm us.

If democracy involves, as Niebuhr claims, accepting proximate solutions for insoluble problems, then "Li'l Abner," by ridiculing formalists and absolutists, is a good democratic strip. If the use of a native vernacular in the form of a romance is part of an American tradition, then "Li'l Abner" is a typically American work. And since it does have a commitment to social and political comment, it does, I believe, yield a great deal of information about American values and American society for those willing to investigate the commonplace and think about the ordinary.

CHAPTER 5

Capp's Graphic Technique: Social Criticism and the Pictorial Image

I

There is nothing new about discussing the relationship that exists between any kind of art and the way it reflects society, but there has not been very much said about the art work of a comic strip in this respect. Histories of caricature are full of illustrations of socially relevant caricatures, cartoons, grotesques, and other similar works that were produced for the ordinary citizen and were meaningful to him, yet when we face the "present"—as scholars and critics—we tend to forget about this level and to dismiss it, in our hunger for explicating the "great," the official, or the "serious."

Aside from a discussion of Capp's style as "naturalistic" by Reuel Denney, there is hardly a thing available on the style of comic strip art. It is ignored because of a number of very obvious limitations: the lines must be simple, and often the draftsmanship is poor; colors, when they are used (for Sunday color supplements) cannot be mixed well enough to create subtle, esthetically pleasing solutions; the strips are printed on cheap paper, glanced at momentarily, and then thrown away. To the artist or the critic, both of whom are generally concerned with that which is beyond the flux of things—and art is, after all, something of a quest for permanence—there seems to be little worth bothering with in comic strips. It is hard to take seriously on Sunday what we will wrap garbage with on Monday.

But if we are to have the "high" seriousness that Matthew Arnold says is so important, perhaps we also ought to have "low" seriousness, and take some of the humbler aspects of life more seriously. Or, at least, we should not categorically refuse to think about them, or to mine them for what might turn out to be valuable. I would also claim that in something like the comic strip, any discussion which does not take into account all the factors must lead to serious distortions. The comic strip is an "impure art" and requires a many-faceted analysis. In a sense, it is a perfect form for inter-disciplinary study: it is a pictorial and literary art (even if, generally speaking, a low-brow one), it usually has some kind of social relevance, it is part of mass communications and has a wide audience. All of these facets must be considered if we are to be able to understand it, evaluate it, and assess it properly.

In this chapter, I shall discuss various aspects of Capp's

pictorial humor such as his use of caricature and the grotesque, his naturalism, his sexy girls, his fascination with faces and identity, his interest in ugliness, and his phallicism, and will relate these subjects to Capp's satire and his critique of American values.

II

In discussing Capp as a caricaturist,[2] I am using the term in the broadest sense of its meaning. It is defined in the dictionary as "grotesque or ludicrous exaggeration, distortion by exaggeration of parts or characteristics," and "ludicrous exaggeration or distortion of the peculiar features of a person, group, people, etc."[3] It is with this last aspect of caricature that I will be most concerned, with what might be called Capp's "social caricature," or his distortions of national character (rather than of particular persons—what could be termed "portrait caricature").

I am impressed by the unity in Capp's multifaceted attack on American social foibles, for if we understand the significance of his various techniques, we find an incredible consistency. For example, I have already commented upon his use of puns in his dialogue. It is interesting to note then, that according to Ernst Kris and E. H. Gombrich, in an article "The Principles of Caricature," some caricatures are "at bottom, nothing but visual puns."[4] In "Li'l Abner," when we have a business tycoon named J. Roaringham Fatback who has the features of a pig, we then have a verbal pun reinforced by a visual one. These two kinds of puns in turn reinforce Fatback's actions, which are pig-like—greedy, voracious, and so forth. It is this continual reinforcement of one quality by another that produces the impact that Capp achieves. We have a character whose name suggests pig, who looks like a pig, and who acts like a pig. You can't help getting "the message" from this remarkably integrated work.

In addition, the caricature, as a distortion of the norm, is in itself a critique of society, of what is accepted and what is official. Thus, on three different levels, we find *formal* criticism, or attacks, on norms: the verbal, with the use of vernacular; the pictorial, with the use of caricature; and the narrative, with the use of grotesquerie. I have used the term "attacks" purposely, for the caricature, like most other forms of the comic, contains an invitation to participate in aggression. As Kris explains this:

> Whereas in dreams, owing to the operation of the primary process, thoughts undergo distortion until they become quite unrecognizable; in wit—and, we may add, in caricature—the distortion is only carried through by half, and is subject to the ego's control; a thought is disguised rather than distorted, its distortion is pressed only so far as is consistent with its remaining intelligible to the firstcomer. Here of course we have again to think of the objection that we have been describing a process not confined to wit and caricature but of general validity (Reik, 1929); nevertheless, since it relates to the social character of comic phenomenon, it acquires a peculiar significance in the present context. For their social character is an essential quality of most forms of the comic: "A new joke runs through the town like the news of a recent victory." And to this simile of Freud's we might add: "A caricature *is* a broadside."

The primary social character of tendentious forms of comic expression appears to be conditioned by two factors: in the first place, another person's approval is used to justify one's own aggression, and furthermore, wit and caricature can be recognized as an invitation to that other person to adopt a joint policy of aggression and regression.[5]

It seems obvious to me that this is a wonderful way for Capp to get rid of his aggressions, bolster his ego, and fill his bank account.

There is an interesting problem that arises when we consider the range of Capp's social caricature, for if everything is distorted, as everything tends to be in the strip, then we should find that we are without a center, that there is no sense of the normal, and as a result the impact of the criticism should be lessened. This is not the case, however, for Capp is creating a "negative pole," which we can contrast with the "positive pole" of our everyday life so that, in a sense, not having a normative character who is always central to the action is a source of strength for Capp, and not a weakness. We are forced to make comparisons between the strip and real life, which is much more significant than comparing different characters in the strip. We are forced to "test" reality by measuring it against what is quite obviously absurd.

Capp also throws in a great deal of portrait caricature, and has included a large number of celebrities during the course of the strip. I think that there are a few reasons for this: In the first place, because he wishes to seem *au courant*; secondly, because people are generally amused by caricatures and feel good about recognizing them. It is somewhat like playing a game, or being a detective. The reader feels a sense of accomplishment from discovering the caricature, and superiority: the famous person is ridiculed while the reader is not. Also, many people judge an artist by how well he is able to draw a likeness, and this caricaturing is one way for Capp to "prove" his talent as a draftsman.

Besides caricaturing other people, Capp often has cari-

135

-catures of himself in the strip, and if we compare early and later self-caricatures, we find that he has continued to exaggerate his features so that he has, in a sense, a new identity. The earlier drawings Capp made of himself were much more "realistic," and had few distortions. But in a caricature that he made of himself at the end of 1964, we find considerable changes: he has aged, his face is puffed up, his nose is bulbous, he is projected as sort of a merry, happy-go-lucky, agrarian type, a country-style comic strip artist who lives in a little log cabin and is friends with all the "folks." His sign says "AL CAPP certified public hill-billy cartoonist." This intensification of his *comic* identity coincides with efforts to be taken "seriously" as a columnist, drama critic, and television personality, rather than as someone who just draws comic strips.

The fact that there is so much purposeful distortion, so much caricature, makes me think that we must seriously qualify any classification of Capp's style as "naturalistic." The style is crude and often heavy handed, to fit in with the tone of the strip, the setting, and the characters. But to call it naturalistic because it is crude is, I believe, to oversimplify matters, and to neglect the symbolism, the humor, and the intellectual qualities it has. I find it hard to see Capp's graphic style as naturalistic. It is, perhaps, best described as a mixed style.

I would add that it is not possible to describe Capp's graphic technique with one term, for there are two very definite conflicting styles in the strip. For one thing, there is the very evident distortion, the caricatures, the bumpkins, the ugly little men and women, the big goofs, who live in a crudely drawn world. On the other hand, there are numerous fairly well drawn young girls in the strip, who often have no relation at all to the action. They are merely passing by.

Self-Caricatures of Capp

Often they are in the foreground while the action and dialogue take place in the background.

I am led, then, to the conclusion that "Li'l Abner" is very much a "girlie" strip. The girls, are, in their own two-dimensional way, sexually stimulating, and help account for much of the popularity of the strip. If the manifest function of "Li'l Abner" is to satirize society, one of the latent functions is to provide sexual stimulation to the male readers. Capp once described how he learned how to please editors. He mentioned that he discovered one editor always liked drawings when they had a girl with her skirt blown up by the wind and her legs showing, and sold many drawings to this editor by using this device. He still uses a variation of it and I believe it is one of the main reasons for the strip's widespread acceptance.

If we recall what Capp said about the ordinary man being somewhat insecure about his masculinity, we can understand the role these girls play in the reader's subconscious. I might note that in "Li'l Abner" we often find little men with big, tall, voluptuous women and, as I have already mentioned, Abner himself is not particularly interested in women, for various reasons. All of this possibly allows the reader to project himself into the various erotic situations: Abner, fool that he is, repels the advances of Daisy Mae and all other voluptuous females. The reader would "know what to do," however; and though he may even be small or insignificant, it doesn't matter, for tall and beautiful women will associate with him, as they do with other characters in the strip. Female readers can project themselves into the various voluptuous young women in the strip and have vicarious thrills of their own.

If all this is true, then the reader of "Li'l Abner" quite possibly is getting a lot for his money: his ego is reinforced by seeing his obvious superiority to the characters in the strip; his political and social education is furthered, with a good deal of attendant moralizing; and his sexual life, in the form of subconscious fantasies, is enriched . . . or at least titillated. There is almost as much "cleavage" in Capp's country girls as in the nudes in *Playboy* magazine.

In addition to all the glamour girls, there is a considerable amount of phallicism in "Li'l Abner." Of course it is easy to find sexual symbolism everywhere, depending upon how hard you are willing to look and how permissive you are willing to be in interpreting long thin objects as penises, and churches and chapels as symbols of women (as Freud does).[6] If one considers the frequent appearances of phallus shaped objects like the Shmoo, the Kigmy, the Snow-ham, and other hams, however, I do think there is a reasonable basis for at least mentioning this matter. Perhaps all these phalli serve to excite female readers, though somewhat more subtly than the way the sexy girls excite males. (Actually I think that this subject should be explored—by a psychiatrist or psychoanalyst, if possible. It might yield remarkable insights.)

There is little question but that some kind of tension exists in the strip—between what we might call sexual excitement and oral satisfaction. Abner and Tiny are more interested in food than sex, which suggests a sort of infantilism on their part. In this respect, their names, curiously enough, are fitting: *Li'l* Abner (little) and *Tiny* (infant) are both quite appropriate to their behavior; or, that is, to their infantile level of development. Thus, when we find Abner eating bananas—as he so often does—it is meant to show that he is somewhat like an ape, but it also reveals he is not very much alive sexually.

Another problem in the same vein is that of identity.

Capp is fascinated by faces, by twins, by people who look like each other (Abner has a double, a gangster named Gat Garson), and by the effect a change in facial features has on character. We can see this in an episode that followed the Snow-ham story and which involved plastic surgery.[7] The "deb of the year," Piper Pincus, was engaged to a famous plastic surgeon, Burl Hives. (Here we have a play on the names of two entertainers: Burl Ives and Piper Laurie.)

As the story starts, Fatback has fired his chauffeur because of his defeat in the Snow-ham trial. He says to himself "I've GOT to take this out on some poor, helpless slob!!" Upon seeing Milton, Roaringham shouts "YOU, MILTON —BLAST YOUR POINTED HEAD—YOU'RE FIRED." Piper Pincus, who happened to be walking by, takes Milton, who becomes her chauffeur, to Hives for plastic surgery. She says to him "LOOK at the poor darling's pitiful little pointed head, and orangutan face!!—only YOUR genius can help him!!" Then she decides he should have "Rock Hudson's nose, Cary Grant's chin, and Fabian's hairline." Milton meanwhile bleats that all he has ever wanted to do was look like a human being—*any* human being. After the operation, Milton emerges as a handsome brute and Piper immediately jilts Hives for him: "What I love about you, Milton—is that you're UNIQUE!! No one else in the WORLD looks like YOU!!" A little later in the story however, when Piper realizes the profundity of Hives' love for her, and sees Milton in his "true light," she returns to Hives. For she thinks to herself: "Hmm!—Ever since MILTON, here, became handsome—HE'S been a selfish, conceited jackass!!" and so she goes back to Hives, "A REALLY NICE MAN!!"

The changes in Milton's face have led to changes in his personality, and he has become—what Capp seems to feel any handsome man *must* be—conceited. We find in this tale that

Cappian Grotesques

JACK JAWBREAKER

CURSE YOUR POINTED HEAD, MILTON!! GET THIS CAR STARTED—INSTANTLY—OR—YOU'RE THROUGH!!

OH, *SOB!* EVERYT'ING'S WOIKIN' POIFECT—EXCEPT IT WON'T BUDGE.!!~

Abner is also conceited, for when Hives says that he is going to make Abner the "handsomest man in the world," he says, "But, ah already IS—." Abner may be pretty stupid—though he isn't above using his brain in desperate situations—but he still is conceited. But handsome men and glamour girls—with the exception of Daisy Mae—do not often play major parts in the strip. The average Dogpatcher, along with many of the other characters, is both physically and temperamentally grotesque.

There is a pattern to Capp's graphic exaggeration. Feet and hands are usually enlarged, bodies are either extended into stringbean-like shapes or short, fat, dumpling-like ones. Most of the caricaturing and grotesquery involve faces, however: noses are enlarged, extended, twisted, made bulbous, or hooked; mouths are enlarged, teeth are taken out or filed into points, lips are made thick and incredibly fleshy, jaws are wildly prognathous, and so on. And Capp takes other liberties, such as parting Abner's hair on whichever side of his face is exposed to the reader. All this reinforces the basic presupposition of the strip—that it is all fantastic, hence, beyond the pale of criticism for its criticisms.

Despite the crudity of the drawings, and they are crude because Capp wants them that way, there is a considerable amount of expression in the faces. The faces of the characters, besides being ugly, register emotion fairly well. Abner generally has a look that is a cross between bewilderment and amazement. Capp achieves this effect by employing a great deal of stylization. Abner, and most of Capp's characters, have eyes that are represented by a dot and a semi-circular line over it—but not under it. Thus, he always seems to be wide-eyed, as if in amazement, especially because his eyes are a bit more exaggerated than those of other characters.

But it is not through eyes that Capp represents emotions—it is through his drawings of mouths. The highly-stylized eyes of Capp's characters hardly reveal any emotion at all, though by using pointing eye-brows and lines on fore-heads, he is able to represent some feeling. However the most obvious indicator of emotion—in real life as well as in the comics—is the mouth, and Capp's mouths are wonderful. Because of his highly stylized presentation of eyes he is lim-ited, for not very much can be done with an eye as he presents it, but he has full freedom in his use of mouths. A look at his faces shows this: the various moods and feelings of the characters characters can generally be interpreted by looking at their mouths.

And like most everything else in "Li'l Abner," the mouths are exaggerated: they are bigger than normal ones, there are often gaps between teeth, and teeth are often pointed. Also, the emotions are as exaggerated as the features of the characters.

There are a number of reasons for all this exaggerated distortion. For one thing, people seem to consider people with big noses, and other somewhat grotesque features, as somehow "funny." Possibly this is because we regard all de-viations from the norm as funny—in the sense of being strange—because we feel superior, in that we have not been distorted, and because we gain relief from anxiety. Accord-ing to Kris, all manifestations of the comic serve this purpose:

> The compromise achieved by the comic is the founda-tion of a phenomenon well-known to psychoanalysts: the comic as a mechanism of defense. We know it from clinical experience; here it can appear in various guises to master and ward off emotions, above all anxiety.[8]

Kris sees the comic as double-edged: it generally causes pleas-ure, but under certain conditions it can cause displeasure and also pain. He gives as an example a joke that falls flat: in this case the aggression involved in humor is exposed and the situation becomes painful. In the same manner, we can look upon Capp's grotesques, and especially one such as Lena the Hyena, as horrible, not funny.

Another reason for the distortions is that Capp can ridicule people, and this is an effective—even if somewhat unethical—way of arguing a position. By making Senator Phogbound three feet tall, Capp visually deflates pomposity, and prepares us for the revelation that Phogbound is corrupt, and a lackey of big business. When Capp makes Roaringham a pig, we know what to expect of him. Incidentally, making a man resemble an animal is a very old device.

C. R. Ashbee, whose book *Caricature* is very much concerned with the social and political implications of caricature, writes:

> When we inquire how the word caricature first comes into use in English we find it is in the eighteenth century, coming to us from Italy, by way of Venice. "When men's faces are drawn with resemblance to some other animals," writes Sir. T. Browne in 1690, "the Italians call it to be drawn in Caricatura." Hogarth uses the word in its English form; and nearly a century later a learned German, Muller, writing on Greek art, uses it as implying a "destruction of beauty and regularity by exaggerated characterising"; "that," says he, or his English translator, "is caricature."
>
> At the back of this is the Platonic idea that perfection of type is attainable on earth, and with it the Aristotelian "golden mean." This Hellenic or humanist ideal the artists and writers of the Classic Renaissance carry through into our own times.[9]

As I interpret this passage, it implies that behind the caricature and the grotesque is what we might term a "classical conception." Caricature is merely an indirect way of preaching the golden mean—instead of giving an example of this mean, it gives an example of something that is both far removed from it and absurd. The ultimate intention, however, is the same: to stress regularity and the "golden mean."

If this is so, to the extent that the golden mean is conservative, so is caricature. In a perverted ambiance, in a society that is insane, the golden mean is radical; in a normal society, it is conservative. But in all cases, it is, by definition, and historically, a decidedly classical conception.

This would lead me to believe that there is a considerable classical dimension to "Li'l Abner." I have already mentioned that the characters tend to be "types," and this is a classical or neo-classical conception. Then, if Ashbee is right, there are the Platonic and Aristotelian implications of caricature—the distortions which suggest the norm. And there are characters like "Pappus," a specific character type from Roman comedy, who is somewhat *transmogrified* into "Pappy" but still retains his old identity.

I find that once again there is a tension set up which is the result of the two ways we can look at the drawings. The "double-edged" quality of the comic strip can be seen here, both in the language and the drawings. We are presented with situations that are ambivalent: the language often has two meanings and the drawings suggest two attitudes. We can see the caricatures both as attacking any given norm and as implying a different one. And just as we can derive either pleasure or pain from a joke, we can read the caricature either as radical or as conservative. Capp is decidedly oracular—he speaks out of both sides of his mouth at once, though in real life he is considered a liberal. (Perhaps this is the definition of a liberal?) [10]

III

The fact that Capp is both a real person *and* a character in the strip is one of the unusual aspects of "Li'l Abner." There is no clear cut distinction possible between the real world and the imaginary one of the strip—characters cross the lines frequently—so rather than reading an unreal strip, we seem to be in touch with life and all its absurdities. In a sense, a comic strip is "alive," for unlike other forms, it develops from day to day and never ends—unless it loses its popularity, or its creator dies and the strip is not continued by a successor. Capp deliberately fuses the world of the characters and the real world, the world of the readers, so that "Li'l Abner" does not seem to be a fiction so much as a distorted report of everyday life. His characters do not pretend they are real, and as a result they seem to be all the more real, especially since *they* read comic strips. The utilization of so many caricatures of famous people supports this illusion.

One other unusual quality of the strip is its fascination with ugliness. I have already mentioned Capp's predilection for the grotesque. The grotesque involves distortion and incongruity, but it need not be ugly, for "ugly" implies "offensive to the sight," "hideous," or "morally repugnant." Capp's grotesques *are*, however, ugly, and their ugliness is incredible, in comparison with other strips. (The only other strip with comparable ugliness is "Dick Tracy.") Strictly speaking, as I have mentioned, there are distinctions that can be made between the caricature, the grotesque, and the ugly, but for my purposes, and especially because of the nature of Capp's style, I have chosen to consider caricature and the grotesque as fundamentally alike. And I think that Capp's grotesques, for the most part, happen to be ugly.

Capp had a contest in which his readers were invited to

draw a face for the ugliest woman in the world, Lena the Hyena, and received almost a million entries. The face that he chose is unquestionably ugly—but it is more than that, it is cruel, it is disgusting. If caricatures are symbols of aggression on the part of their makers, then this face represents aggression of awe-inspiring intensity and is almost pathological.

And yet, at the same time, we have the never-ending succession of glamour girls (who in their own way—their bulging breasts, for instance—are somewhat grotesque themselves). I think that what we have here is typical of the strip: a dialectic, a tension that exists because of pulls in opposing directions, and we find all this presented both verbally and pictorially. We have Capp's dialogue, but we also have his images—and the images, just as well as his words, "present" ideas that are emotionally gripping and have content.

If we recall that the second meaning of "ugliness" is "offensive from a moral aspect," then we can see that ugliness, like the grotesque, is an appeal to ideas. It is a mark of realism on Capp's part—he refuses to forget about the commonplace, about that which really is ugly and unpleasant, and if he goes overboard in his presentations, if he goes to extremes to remind us of the existence of the ugly, it is because he is forced to do so. We try so hard to believe that it does not exist, that it is not important, that sometimes we fool ourselves. It is worth noticing that in presenting ugly, poor, and stupid people in his strip, he is running smack against one of the conventions of the American mass media, which project a view of middle class opulence as being universal.

There is one episode in the strip that deals with poor people and is significant for a number of reasons. In the story, Abner has been mistaken for Gat Garson by a group of Chicago gangsters and told that he will be "knocked off" in a couple of weeks. Marryin' Sam, opportunist that he is, decides to take advantage of this by taking out a policy on Abner with the "Last Round-Up" insurance company, which will pay $100,000 in the event of his sudden death. To get money for the first payment, every Dogpatcher has to mortgage his house (including the Yokums, though Mammy is away and Pappy is gulled into it, not knowing who is involved).

The Dogpatchers are shown to be rather callous and not particularly decent human beings. When they first hear that the gangsters are going to kill Abner they all start crying; then Marryin' Sam has his brainchild:

MARRYIN SAM: One moment folks!! Thar IS some hope!!

DOGPATCHERS: ?!! Yo' means "th' boys" might NOT knock him off?

MARRYIN SAM: Oh, they'll knock him off all right—but WE all stands t'clean up $100,000.00 on th' deal!!

DOGPATCHERS: YIPPAY! HOORAY FO' LI'L ABNER!! Allus knowed he'd amount t' something!! Namely $100,000!

MARRYIN SAM: Ah don't know WHY "th' boys" is gonna "knock off" Li'l Abner, come noo y'ars eve—an' frankly ah DON'T CARE! Main thing is, ef we DON'T insure him fo' $100,000.00 — HIS DEATH WILL BE A TURRIBLE LOSS TO US!!

149

Mammy Yokum returns but is unable to do anything. The Dogpatchers throw a banquet for Abner, but since they have no money it is a very threadbare affair. And then, with a target attached to his chest, Abner goes up on top of a mountain to wait for the boys. He is a living target, so to speak. To make things easier for the gangsters, the Dogpatchers have posted signs telling "the boys" where he is.

Unfortunately for the Dogpatchers, the gangsters find out that Abner is not Gat Garson. When Abner discovers this he shouts for joy, "YIPPAY!! Ah is gonna LIVE!!" to which Marryin' Sam replies "Thass th' worst news Dogpatch EVEH had—an' HE'S happy 'bout it!!"

The whole story hinges on the matter of mistaken identity, but there are a couple of other important issues: the depravity of the Dogpatchers and the question of the relationship that exists between the individual and society. The myth of agrarian goodness and innocence is attacked in this story. The Dogpatchers are shown to be terribly selfish and reprehensible people. We can expect this if we recall that Capp sees the victims of oppression as becoming degraded themselves. Given this social temperament, we can expect the political order to be anarchistic, and it is. In this example, the various Dogpatchers were able to unite because they foresaw immediate personal advantage; ordinarily, however, life is chaotic. Dogpatch is a matriarchy, ruled over by Mammy and her lieutenant, Abner.

This is made clear in another story in which the following dialogue takes place:

MAMMY: Money hain't everything!! RESPECK!! Thass what counts!! We is pore as rats— but we gits more respeck than a barrel o' monkeys!!—All our neighbors looks UP t'us WIF ADMY-RAY-SHUN AN' FEAR!!

PAPPY: NATCHERLY!!—ef' 'twarn't fo' th' fightin' abilities o' YO' dear—an' Li'l Abner—it wouldn't be safe for NOBODY t' live in Dogpatch.

ABNER: RIGHT!!—Mammy an' me is th' strongest critters in all these hills!!—Nobody DASTS harm no Dogpatcher while WE is around!!

Capp's political philosophy and his psychology of humor are both Hobbesian, as I have mentioned above, and here we can see how the two theories complement each other. In Dogpatch, where the ego is absolute, politics must be based on power; especially since there is no intelligence. The characters are physically ugly and morally ugly—their values are as perverse as their faces. The whole conception is remarkably integrated; despite the crudity and the absurdity there is a unity and sense to the world of "Li'l Abner," once we accept the "givens" of the strip.

In discussing "Li'l Abner" I have had to mediate between an analysis of specific qualities of the strip and an explanation of certain formal qualities of comic strips in general; therefore, besides talking about what Capp's caricature of a voracious businessman means, I have also discussed the meaning of caricature in general. I feel that this has been necessary because of the peculiar nature of this study, in which so many different disciplines have been utilized and in which relationships that I found intriguing forced me into explanations and explications that tend to be discursive. In the next chapter, which terminates this study, I shall discuss the relevance and usefulness of an interdisciplinary approach to an analysis of "Li'l Abner" and American society, and offer a compressed and unified presentation of my main conclusions.

CHAPTER 6

Conclusions

I

There is something almost perverse about my having written a study of "Li'l Abner." I can remember that before I came to the University of Minnesota I had a discussion about American Studies with my brother, Jason, a painter, who had taught at a number of universities in the Boston area. "American Studies," he said, "is a Shmoo. If you bake it, it's history; if you broil it, it's literature; if you fry it, it's philosophy." I can't help thinking that these words were continually ringing in the back of my head as I wrote this dissertation. But there is more. Demonstrating, at least to my satisfaction, that he has picked up a good deal of academic jargon, he continued, "forget about all this interdisciplinary stuff. What you want to do is profound yourself in a dis-cipline."

The conversation moved on to other subjects, but he had articulated what are perhaps the central issues involved in any discussion of interdisciplinary studies: the question of who has "property rights" to a subject and the suggestion that an interdisciplinary study must be superficial, not "profound." What is unfortunate about all this is that there are no answers to disputes about "terrains." Should a history of political philosophy be taught in a history course, a philosophy course, or a political science course? Good arguments could be made for all three disciplines "owning" this subject, but the most important consideration, I think, is where the emphasis is to be put: on the historical, the philosophical, or the political.

The same holds true, I would say, with the matter of interdisciplinary and single-disciplinary studies. In interdis-ciplinary studies, there is a conscious and explicit recognition that the academic boundaries which exist are only conveniences. I would venture to suggest that it is frequently almost impossible, except for highly technical investigations, to remain in *one* discipline, and most people are beginning to recognize this. A look at a book like Ferdinand Lot's *The End of the Ancient World and The Beginnings of the Middle Ages* provides a good example of what I mean. In this book, which was written by a distinguished historian, we find dis-cussions of philosophy, literature, economics, politics, and art, just to mention a few disciplines.

It might be argued that this is a good example of some-one who has "profounded" himself in his discipline, but I think that this position cannot be supported. What it amounts to saying is that knowing something about other disciplines is important, but that such knowledge be implicit in one's training, not explicit. At this point we have abandoned discussing whether or not interdisciplinary approaches are valid, and are now disputing *how* we can best prepare for this kind of approach.

I mention this matter of interdisciplinary approaches to subjects because in my own case, this investigation of "Li'l Abner," there is no other adequate approach. The strip has so many different aspects that needed to be discussed that I was forced to employ a number of different disciplines. How else could I have come to grips with the art work, the narrative style, the language, the historical backgrounds of American satire, and the wide range of subjects involved in the strip? I have used literary criticism to discuss the language, the narrative style, and the formal elements of Capp's satire. I have used historical analysis to place "Li'l Abner" in American satire and explain the strip's frame of reference. I have gone to psychology for an understanding of the mechanisms behind caricature and humor, in general, and for "informed guesses" about the significance of certain characters and events in "Li'l Abner." I have drawn upon political science to explore the political implications of certain aspects of the strip, such as the role of the expert, the relation that exists between the individual and society, and the Hobbesian nature of Capp's theory of humor and political theory.

The possibilities in "Li'l Abner" for interdisciplinary analysis have been recognized by other scholars. For example, Orrin E. Klapp mentions a number of different aspects of Capp's social criticism that he finds in one episode, that of the Zoot-Suiters. He makes a distinction between "personal mockery" and "type mockery," namely that "the first punished a person for failure to live up to the norm but the second punishes a *norm*, so to speak—that is, throws into question an ideal, a role, or even an entire structure."[1]

Conclusions

Despite the various disciplines that I have used, I must admit to a feeling of inadequacy. It is difficult to deal with contemporary subjects, let alone a subject that quite literally is continually growing, day-by-day. Of course the artist is not present to the same degree in all his works, so by concentrating upon certain episodes that are, I feel, significant and representative, I have been able to discover something about the strip and to come to some conclusions about it.

II

The purpose of this study has been to evaluate Capp as an artist and to see how his work reflects certain aspects of American society. I find him complex and integrated, taking advantage of the opportunities rather than being hamstrung by the limitations of his medium. His verbal and graphic puns, for instance, serve to reinforce each other and help sustain his irony. I also think his imagination and sense of invention are quite incredible. And, in addition to exploiting the American vernacular and a certain type of folksy-art ("Li'l Abner" is not folk art but pseudo-folk art), Capp's interests have generally been public—social and political.

Capp is, unquestionably, one of the most durable of contemporary American satirists—and probably one of the most important, at least in terms of the size of his audience. For more than thirty years he has been satirizing American society, writing, as he puts it, the equivalent of two novels a year.

One of the most puzzling questions about American culture is why we have so little satire, or at least political satire. We have always had a good deal of social satire—the *New Yorker* and other magazines are always full of cutting cartoons about the various absurdities of American life. But there has not been until recently—that is, with the rise of the oral commentators, an American version of the French chansoniers—a great deal of significant political satire.

Part of the reason for this, suggests the *New Republic* theater critic, is that we have no "ruling class":

> Despite the serio-comic efforts of Richard Rovere to uncover one, there is no American Establishment, only a changing guard of Influentials rising periodically from a multitude on the make. A true Establishment—based as it is on order, tradition, and hierarchy—exists independently of favor or fashion, but our power structure is a moving target which is always changing its outline. I mention this in partial explanation of why English satire is political and ours is not—since we have no ruling classes, there is never sufficient distance established between the electorate and its representatives. . . . American political satire seems to cope effectively only with generals, Southern senators, and FBI agents—that is to say, with men who are able to jar the satirist out of his political apathy into genuine indignation.[2]

Another reason probably has something to do with the climate of opinion here in America. Although, earlier in our history, we had savage political satirists, the American political ethos seems to have developed a halo, and attacks upon it, and upon political figures, are often taken to be "anti-American."

Arthur M. Schlesinger Jr. mentions this in *The Politics of Hope*. He says:

> The new atmosphere is no longer conducive to the old escapes. To satirize the American businessman today, for example, is to invite suspicion and attack; what was once satiric is now (in the business community, at least) subversive. . . . The most brilliant and daring of our comic

strip cartoonists, Al Capp, finally had to marry off his two leading characters, because, no longer feeling himself free to "kid hell out of everything," he felt he had no choice but to convert knockabout satire into a fairy story. "For the first 14 years [of the strip] I reveled in the freedom to laugh at America. But now America has changed. The humorist feels the change more, perhaps, than anyone. Now there are things about America we can't kid."[3]

Capp explained why he turned "Li'l Abner" into a family, domestic comedy strip in an interview that appeared in *The New Yorker*. It was not because most of the fan letters he received wanted the marriage, though this happened to be true, but because of the McCarthy period:

McCarthy was coming to power when I created shmoos, and those were inconceivably terrible times. They got worse and worse, until eventually the only satire possible and permissible in this democracy of ours was broad, weak domestic comedy. That's why I married off Li'l Abner and began to concentrate on him again. . . .[4]

It is, perhaps, debatable as to how much specifically *political* satire there is in "Li'l Abner." What Brustein said about American political satire taking on cream puffs seems to apply to Capp. But there is more to Capp's satire than Southern senators and social comment. He attacks, with a sense of moral indignation, such controversial subjects as the medical profession, foreign aid, and the Cold War. What is problematical about Capp is that so much of his indignation is *moral*, that he appeals for a change in heart more than a change in political structure.

The problem, as I see it, is that there is a paradox involved in the nature of *political* satire: if the comment is too specific and too involved in concrete solutions to wrongs, it becomes political theory; if the comment is too broad, it loses its intensity. Or, to put it in other words, a satirist who is merely negative, who functions only to pull down, who has nothing positive to offer, can be criticized for being half-hearted, no matter how savage his satire—for he has nothing to offer in the way of alternatives.[5] And yet, if a satirist offers specific alternatives (that can be taken seriously) he must abandon a good deal of satire, otherwise we will *not* take him seriously.

I do not think that Capp has resolved this tension, or that any satirist can resolve it. Calling for a change in heart may, in its own way, be as revolutionary as making specific proposals about foreign relations and government spending. What Capp does, I believe, is to suggest change by ridiculing what he sees before him. It is very difficult to do much more, especially with a comic strip. The only reason that Capp gets away with as much as he does is that "Li'l Abner" *is* a comic strip. Abner is a fool and like the medieval fool can get away with many things.

In a study of what might be called satirical "temperament," Leonard Feinberg offers support for my idea that political satire involves a dilemma. Instead of looking at the work, he says, we should understand the motivations of the political satirist and his techniques. He adds:

> In discussing the politics of satirists it is well to remember that by his very nature, the satirist is an attacker rather than a defender. Criticism functions by exposing the wrong rather than praising the right. For the satirist it is less a problem of morality than of temperament and technique.[6]

Satire forces a writer to be critical—indeed, Feinberg's definition of satire is *"a playfully critical distortion of the fa-*

miliar"[6]—so that being constructive must take a back seat to being "destructive." And it may just be that cleaning any Augean stables of the mind is, in its own way, a positive contribution to society.

We must also deal with the problem of how truly "Li'l Abner" represents or reflects American culture: that is, how much of it is some kind of mirror and how much of it is merely Capp's own picture of America. There is no sure way to resolve this particular question, for in any work of art there is always the matter of "the forming hand" and the taste of the creator. But the vast popularity of "Li'l Abner" suggests that quite probably it does strike home, that it does mean something to the average reader, and that in itself is, I would say, significant.

I would add that I do not think the reader of "Li'l Abner" uses it as an escape mechanism but precisely in the opposite way—as a way of encountering and interpreting experience: of learning about human nature, of seeing into political chicanery, and so forth. The lessons may be masked by exaggeration and fantasy, but to a large degree all this represents only a sugar-coating of the didactic pill. The fact that "Li'l Abner" focuses on society and social and political problems suggests this. The very first adventure in "Li'l Abner" involved a satirization of New York "high society" and Capp has continually trained his guns on issues of public interest for more than thirty years. Capp, then, is popular precisely because he does *not* lose sight of the "reality principle," and is in touch with the concerns of the day.

Despite Capp's move into situation comedy, there have not been many really important changes in his technique over the past thirty years. His narratives have the same basic structure, although his imagination and sense of fantasy have matured somewhat. We find the same comic ingenuity at the beginning of the strip that we find now. For example, one of the earliest adventures in "Li'l Abner" found him caught in a vicious cycle: he had wandered into a high-class restaurant to eat and had a large meal. Then he discovered he didn't have enough money to pay for the meal and had to wash dishes. However, after washing dishes for a while he got hungry and had another meal. He then had to wash more dishes—and on and on the cycle went, until he was rescued by his mother—who discovered where he was by a magic vision.

Capp's drawing is better now. It is less crude and less realistic. His line is surer and more fluid. His early figures tended to be stiff, and movement was presented somewhat awkwardly. The faces of his characters and their bodies have generally changed somewhat, and his animals are no longer amateurish. There has been a decided movement in his work toward stylistic distortion, both in the representation of people and of landscape, in fantastic creations and in what we might call the "Cappian sensibility." Abner has changed from a rather beaver-faced adolescent to a mature and generally handsome masculine figure, and Daisy Mae to a voluptuous "sexpot." In addition, the dialogue is more emphatic—there are two exclamation marks instead of one and many more words in heavy print. But changes like this are to be expected as an artist develops his technique and they have not been, I would say, fundamental. The strip is more stylized, but fundamentally the same as it was in the beginning.

As an aid in understanding the significance of Capp's work in this respect, there is much of interest in the comments of Henry James on caricature:

> As we attempt, at the present day, to write the history of everything, it would be strange if we had happened to neglect the annals of caricature; for the very

Li'l Abner: 1936 and 1965

essence of the art of Cruikshank and Gavarni, or Daumier and Leech, is to be historical; and every one knows how addicted is this great science to discoursing about itself. Many industrious seekers, in England and France, have ascended the stream of time to follow to its source the modern movement of pictorial satire. The stream of time is in this case mainly the stream of journalism; for social and political caricature, as the present century has practised it, is only journalism made doubly vivid.

The subject is a large one, if we reflect upon it, for many people would tell us that journalism is the greatest invention of our age. If this rich branch has shared the great fortune of the parent stream, so, on other sides, it touches the fine arts, touches manners and morals. All this helps to account for its inexhaustible life; journalism is the criticism of the moment *at* the moment, and caricature is that criticism at once simplified and intensified by a plastic form.[7]

It is well to remember that "Li'l Abner" is a particular kind of journalism and pictorial satire. Since journalism is generally associated with that which is transitory and superficial, quite possibly this brings to light some hidden reason for deprecating the comics.

Seen in this light, I would suggest that comics are what might be called a "documentary art," and as such must be treated as both document and art. If we understand this, we can avoid excoriating the comics for not doing what they are not meant to do and cannot possibly do.

III

To complicate matters further, I find many of the same tensions in Capp that I find in American society, so that his "dilemma" is only a reflection of a much larger set of dilemmas. It is fashionable now to characterize American thought as involving a "dialogue" between conflicting political, economic, and other positions. These conflicts are the proof of our pluralistic pudding. Thus I find that Capp is both fascinated and terrified by the business hero, just as most Americans are; we worship material success yet feel that wealth corrupts. Capp's tycoon, General Bullmoose, for example, is a rogue, but he has an intensity that is fascinating, and he makes most of his money on human foolishness.

In the same manner, Capp is basically pragmatic and non-ideological, yet he does not want to give up absolute values. In an episode involving Bald Iggles, Capp upheld absolute values and favored doing what was "right" even if it was illegal. The adventure involved Mammy Yokum protecting little creatures called Bald Iggles, who make people tell the truth. In the story, Mammy has sent Abner, Daisy Mae, and Honest Abe into the woods with a Bald Iggle to protect him from being destroyed. The following dialogue takes place between Mammy and Blugstone, a detective:

MAMMY: Li'l Abner done took th' Bald Iggle outa yore murderin' reach!!

BLUGSTONE: But protecting one of those creatures is ILLEGAL!!

MAMMY: Illegal!! Shmillegal!! As long as what he's doin' is right—thas all AH cares about!![8]

There is also the tension between Capp's realism, which shows us how hollow and absurd is so much that we tend to take seriously, and his romanticism. He mocks the ideal of agrarian innocence and goodness, yet I cannot help feeling he would like to believe in it and is trying to convince himself. He is pessimistic about human goodness, yet he appeals to it, as, for example, in the conclusion to his first Shmoo story when he pleads for a change in heart in people. I think there is a great deal of pessimism and cynicism in the strip. Goodness is an ideal not attainable by man, it seems; an ideal ironically hinted at through Capp's presentation of human selfishness and ugliness.

"Li'l Abner" itself bears out this conclusion. The strip is, to a great degree, a study in villainy and villains. Most of the characters are either ignorant or vicious, and some are both. In addition, Capp ridicules popular heroes, professions (such as politics, medicine, the military, the police, entertainers), popular culture, and even other comic strips.

We might see Abner as anti-hero. After all, he is a fool, he has no profession, and he is embarrassingly uninterested in women. He is a man without qualities in a world that is without order, without sanity, and in moral and political chaos. He is a continual refutation of the American dream of rising from rags to riches—for he always is in rags and seems to be happy there. In the final analysis, he is good for nothing but a laugh.

To a large degree, "Li'l Abner" reflects what I would call the "sour side" of Puritanism, the sense of depravity and guilt that is, unfortunately, too often seen as *all* of Puritanism. But he also reflects the other side of Puritanism, the satiric impulse that we find in a writer like Benjamin Tompson and the realism, the interest in subjects that are "low" and materials that might be considered trivial, that we find in so many of the Puritan writers. Also, in Puritan writing we find a good deal of fantasy and word play, we find fools, and a wide range of allusion. The great-great-grandaddy of Abner may well have been Nathaniel Ward's "hero" of *The Simple Cobbler of Aggawam*, though there are, naturally, numerous differences between the two characters.

We also find in Puritanism the same tension between

individualism and the group, the same distrust of political authority, and the same belief in absolutes—in Natural Law.[9] Curiously enough, we also find the beginnings of the conflict that was to grow into what we have now between mass culture and high culture, though with different terms. I am referring to the struggle between what is called "plain style" versus "perspicuous style" in writing, and a bit later in "regular singing" versus "the folk tradition" in singing. I think that without too much stretching we can see what was originally "plain style," that which was available to all, which did not require a great deal of education and sophistication, growing into popular culture, once the proper technological developments came. The same holds true of music, according to Gilbert Chase's *America's Music*:

> It is important to understand the conditions under which psalmody and hymnody developed in New England during the eighteenth century and to comprehend, in particular, the nature of the divergent and conflicting cultural trends that made New England a virtual battle-ground between the zealous reformers who advocated and tried to impose "Regular Singing," and the common folk who preferred their own way of singing, handed down by oral tradition. The reformers, most of whom were clergymen educated at Harvard, held that "the usual way of singing" practiced by the people was an abomination and an offense against good taste.[10]

The perspicuous style in writing and regular singing, then, developed into "high" culture as we know it now, and the same arguments against the people that were used then seem to be used now.

Seen with this perspective, then, it is not surprising that "Li'l Abner," the comics, and the popular arts in general, are liked by the common folk and seen as "an abomination and offence against good taste" by certain elements of society. It is no longer permissible to call the people a great beast, but it is still all right to tell them that their taste is beastly. To my mind, despite the dubious validity of the esthetics, this is a sign of considerable progress.

IV

Like all studies, this one is incomplete. I regard it as an exploratory one, an attempt to enlarge critical horizons. Because of this, I have been rather polemical, I have often had to be arbitrary, and I have had to be somewhat discursive in my attempt to explicate "Li'l Abner" and to provide a method and rationale for analyzing comic strips in general.

Although "Li'l Abner" is, in my opinion, one of the most important of American comic strips, there is still much to be done—with comics in general and with "Li'l Abner" in particular. For example, the relation between the comic strip and pop art might be developed. Historically orientated scholars might choose to explore the relation between "Li'l Abner" and certain events in American history more fully. I have limited my attention to the comic strip, but Capp's abortive role as a columnist might be studied, as well as his drama criticism, his articles, and his news broadcasting (on the B.B.C. and as a summer replacement for Drew Pearson). Students of the theater might write something about the musical comedy success of "Li'l Abner," and students of mass communications might be able to make something of the vast returns Capp got in his contest for a face for Lena the Hyena. Also, there needs to be a good deal more work on the "theoretical" aspects of comic strips, on their style and the relation to other types of literary and artistic expression.

Finally, I see studies of comic strips and other forms of

popular culture as a preliminary to a much larger field involving what I call "commonplaces." I think that we need to be more catholic in our tastes and in our studies, and along with investigating "classics" we need to look seriously at commonplaces.

I find the comments made about Capp by Herbert Marshall McLuhan in *The Mechanical Bride* very much to the point:

> His keen eye for political, commercial, and social humbug is the result of a critical intelligence which is notably lacking at the more respected levels of writing.
>
> Capp looks at the disordered world around him not as a social reformer who imagines that much good would result from a few changes in external features of business and political administration; he sees these situations refracted through the deeply willed deceptions which every person practices upon himself. The criticism which is embedded in his highly parabolic entertainment, therefore, has a complexity which is the mark of vision. He moves in a world of many dimensions, each of which includes and reflects upon the other.[11]

The existence of a comic strip like "Li'l Abner" convinces me that the possibilities in the popular arts are not as limited as they might seem to be, in regard to both artistic qualities and cultural relevance. I have tried to rescue the comic strip and Capp from relative obscurity (as far as serious scholarly criticism is concerned); and to show that in them we can find both intelligence and imagination functioning in an idiom embodying stylistic conventions that are typically American, and having cultural implications that are significant.

Afterword

In 1963 I was a graduate student in the Ph. D. program in American Studies at the University of Minnesota. I had completed my course work—I did most of my work with David Noble (American Intellectual History), Ralph Ross (Social Thought) and Mulford Q. Sibley (Political Theory). Sibley had agreed to be my advisor, and I was searching for a subject for my dissertation. I was interested in utopian societies, and, for a while, I thought I might work in that area. But I ended up with a comic strip, *Li'l Abner*.

I had, by chance, met Capp in the mid-fifties. His daughter was, at the time, a painting student of my brother Jason (at the Museum of Fine Arts School of Art in Boston), and she was having a party. I went to it, in Cambridge, not realizing that the young woman hosting the party was Capp's daughter. He was there, and I spent a good deal of time chatting with him. Capp was, during those years, associated with the liberal intelligentsia of Cambridge and had not yet become a political reactionary. At the time I was working on my master's degree in the School of Journalism at the University of Iowa. I had no notion then that I would be continuing on and working for a doctorate at the University of Minnesota, or that, of all things, I would write on *Li'l Abner*.

I had written a paper on *Li'l Abner* in Sibley's course in modern American political thought, and we decided it would be best if I took that subject and turned it into a dissertation. My decision to work on *Li'l Abner* was seen by my fellow students in the American Studies program as frivolous, if not ridiculous. At that time the notion of doing a doctoral dissertation on a comic strip was most unusual, and the committee of professors that reviewed thesis proposals gave me a good deal of difficulty over the matter. There was, I learned later, a split between the humanities professors, who didn't think the topic was suitable, and the social science professors, who liked the idea. Sibley had an enormous amount of prestige and was able to get the subject accepted.

But I had to revise my dissertation description to suit everyone on the committee, and that took a good deal of doing. I have notes in my journals about my problems in figuring out what to do with *Li'l Abner* and how to structure my study. One of the members of the dissertation committee, J. C. Levenson, a literature professor, made me do a great deal of thinking about how to organize it, but by doing that he turned out to be enormously helpful.

I figured out that it made sense to deal with the essential components of a humorous comic strip: the art style, the language, its narrative aspects, social and political themes, and the relation between the strip and American literature. But how does one deal with a strip that had been appearing for more than thirty years? I decided to focus on some of the more important characters and what I considered to be typical episodes. In hindsight, my notions about how to study comic strips seem perfectly obvious, but in 1963, with little to guide me, I had to struggle to work out my methodology. There were some scholarly articles on comic strips, but they tended to focus on social and political aspects of strips, which was helpful, but not enough to sustain a dissertation length study of a comic strip. And there were some books, such as Coulton Waugh's survey *The Comics*, but they dealt with the comics in general, and not one strip.

I ought to point out that I have always been interested in humor and that I am a cartoonist and writer of humorous prose and verse, so analyzing a humorous comic strip was, in a certain sense, a natural subject for me. For others, as I mentioned above, the idea of doing a dissertation on a comic strip seemed far-fetched, to put it mildly. I can recall vividly what happened at graduation, in 1965.

When we received our hoods at commencement our dissertation titles were announced. A number of typical dissertation titles, on various arcane but acceptable scientific and other subjects, preceded mine. When my title, "Li'l Abner," was announced, many people in the audience laughed.

My first public appearance as a scholar was connected to laughter—the result, perhaps, of astonishment—and was, it turns out, to typify the reactions, in future years, of many people to my work. Laughter, questions came about whether I was serious or not (that is, was I putting people on?), and, in some cases, ridicule. The classic review of my work in popular culture was written by Jeff Greenfield. In a review of my book *The TV-Guided American* he wrote "Berger is to the study of television what Idi Amin is to tourism in Uganda." I use it all the time in my lectures, and it never fails to get a good laugh. Thus ridicule, insulting book reviews, and "put downs" are nothing new to me, and being an iconoclast and a humorist myself (an eiron in Northrop Frye's typology), I thrive on it.

The very first sentence in *Li'l Abner* reads "They laughed

when I sat down at the typewriter!" I was talking about my fellow students. They also laughed when I got up from the typewriter, but I had the last laugh, and the best one, when my dissertation was published by Twayne in 1970.

At the end of the 1962–63 academic year I had completed my course work and passed my exams. All that remained was the dissertation. I was fortunate to win a Fulbright to teach in Italy during the 1963–1964 year, so I took a year off and went to Italy. I had suggested a project on the Italian magazine press, and so I was sent to Milan, the center of publishing in Italy. I was asked to teach two courses at the University of Milan in the American literature program being directed, at that time, by Professor Agostino Lombardo. He later moved to the University of Rome.

I taught two courses: one on Puritan literature and *The Scarlet Letter* and another on Emerson and *Huckleberry Finn*. I had two small classes, and the work wasn't terribly demanding. My students were very much interested in American culture in general and were always fascinated by my descriptions of everyday life in America. I told them about my interest in comics, and they found that perfectly reasonable. When I asked them who was "interesting" in Milan, they all gave the same answer—Umberto Eco.

He was, it turns out, writing about comics and popular culture himself, so I called him, made an appointment to meet in the Galleria, and we became good friends. He hung around with a group of intellectuals who were very serious about popular culture, and I can recall long discussions with him and his friends about camera work in various American television shows and that kind of thing. In 1964 he published a book of essays, *Apocalittici E Integrati*, on mass communications and the theory of mass culture that had two long articles on the comics: one a frame-by-frame analysis of a page from *Steve Canyon* and another on "The Myth of Superman." Eco had not become an internationally known novelist at the time, but he was extremely well known in Italy as a semiotician and critic and was a force on the cultural scene there.

From the Italians I learned that studying the comics was not only acceptable but important, and I discovered a number of scholarly books written by Italian academics on the subject. I became convinced that popular culture was important and that dismissing it as "sub-literary junk" that had no impact on individuals or society, which was the position of many literary scholars, was a big mistake.

Agostino Lombardo published a journal, *Studi Americani*, and asked me to write an article for it on American and Italian comics. Being in Milan I was able to talk with many editors who published comics or books about comics and came up with a list of a half dozen or so of the most important Italian comic strips. A number of these strips were reprinted in a large book with handsome color reproductions of comics from many countries called *I Primi Eroi* (The First Heroes). It was published in 1962 by Garzanti in Milan. One of the editors at Garzanti was a fan of the comics and decided to publish the book.

Once I had my list of classic Italian comics, I then decided to match these comics—in terms of what the heroes or main figures were like and when the comics appeared—with a list of American comics that were similar to the Italian ones. The American strips appeared, roughly, around the same time as the Italian ones and had the same kind of heroes or heroines.

When I examined what I considered to be representative samples of the two sets of comics, I discovered something extremely interesting. The Italian comics saw authority as valid and portrayed a stratified society in which those at the top dominated those beneath them, and this domination was seen, in the strips, as legitimate and acceptable. But the American strips

173

were different. American strips were anti-authoritarian. Rebellion against authority was seen as valid and often successful— lesser figures on the great chain of being often bested their superiors.

Let me offer an example. There was an Italian strip about a soldier, *Marmittone*, that I contrasted with the American strip *Beetle Bailey*. The time periods when they appeared overlapped. Marmittone always gets into trouble or does something stupid and ends up, in the last panel, in prison, with a beam of light on him, highlighting, one might say, his guilt. But Beetle Bailey, low man on the totem pole in his strip, frequently ends up besting his superiors—most of whom are fools or gluttons, and in some cases, such as the Sergeant, both. These strips reflected, I suggested, different attitudes towards authority.

I also investigated research by Italian sociologists on the Italian family and discovered that these families were, in the period leading to the sixties at least, highly authoritarian. There was reason to believe, then, that comic strips were useful indicators of cultural values and beliefs about authority and various other matters.

I wrote an article for Agostino Lombardo's journal and also used the research I did for the article in my first chapter of *Li'l Abner*, where I dealt with popular culture and comics. A version of this article, "Authority in the Comics," was published in *Transaction* (now *Society*) in December of 1966. That was my first American publication.

I returned from Italy in 1964 to write my dissertation on *Li'l Abner* with a sense that comic strips were important and worth studying. My year in Italy had been enormously enriching and exciting. I had done some research that I could use in my discussion of theoretical matters. And I had sketched out in my mind, and in countless notes I had written in my journals, what I would deal with in my dissertation.

In contemporary parlance, *Li'l Abner* is a literary (or some would say sub-literary) narrative text—a creative work—that poses interesting and difficult problems for critics. I alluded to some of these earlier. Analyzing a particular work—a novel or a play—is difficult enough. How was I to deal meaningfully with a comic strip that started in 1934 and had been running for thirty years at the time I decided to write about it?

Obviously it is impossible to deal with every one of Abner's adventures in this vast meta-narrative, or every character. I had to select certain episodes that struck me as particularly interesting and deal with those characters in the strip that I felt to be of paramount importance, from a symbolic point of view. I also wanted to deal with this text contextually in two ways. First, I wanted to see what it reflected about American culture and society and second, I wanted to see how *Li'l Abner* related, intertextually, to American humor (including comic strips), in general, and conventions found in southwestern literary humor, in particular.

Criticism is, we must remember, an art and not a science of interpretation; the use of various disciplines to explicate a text relies, in the final analysis, on the quality of the argument the critic makes. In approaching my task I wanted to avoid the problems caused by the two dominant approaches that were popular at the time. One was a social-scientific one that saw a text as a source of information about values, beliefs, and other socio-cultural phenomena, with little concern for aesthetic considerations. The other was an essentially aesthetic approach. It focused attention on how authors achieved their effects and concerned itself with matters such as plot, theme, characterization, and language, with little concern for social, political, and cultural aspects of a particular text. I wanted to avoid the Scylla of narrow social scientific approaches and the Charybdis of hermetic literary criticism approaches, both of which were, in my opinion, reductionistic.

Many literary critics, to this day, feel that dealing with what they deem to be extra-literary dimensions of a text is a mistake. Let me cite, as an example, Ejner J. Jensen, who writes in *Shakespeare and the Ends of Comedy*: ". . . critics inevitably confuse the task of the playwright with other roles: moralist, counselor, psychologist. Only a short while ago, it seems, this point was so widely accepted as to seem self-evident. The work of art, self-contained and complete, did not and could not depend for its understanding on matters whose existence lay outside itself" (1991, 20). Jensen argues here that a work is to be interpreted in aesthetic and literary terms and nothing else. Psychological matters, ethical concerns, and political considerations are, it is suggested, irrelevant. At the other extreme are those critics who are not interested in the text as a work of creative art but only, it seems, in the way it can be used to deal with interests they have. Thus, Marxist critics focus on ideological matters connected with the text, psychoanalytic critics deal with the unconscious motivations of the characters and the impact the text might have on its readers or viewers, and feminist critics tend to be concerned, essentially, with the way the text portrays women and the impact the text has on issues related to women.

These approaches strike me as unacceptable alone, and I would argue that we must see texts as having both literary and sociopolitical dimensions and that, further, aesthetic matters, such as the form and style of a text, have social and political implications. The first sentence of my "Introduction" makes this point explicitly: "This study begins where other analyses of the comics have generally ended: with a serious and detailed examination of style and the way it is related to meaning." I could not know then that my interest in meaning was to lead me into semiotics, which concerns itself, when it deals with literary and artistic works, with how meaning is generated. Meaning, we must remember, is something that people must find in texts, and as contemporary reader-response critics keep pointing out, the readers of texts—whether they be novels or comic strips—help, in a sense, create the works by bringing whatever knowledge base they have to the texts they are reading.

I was astonished at the fact that a text such as *Li'l Abner*, that was read each day by hundreds of millions of people, was virtually ignored by critics, though there were some random articles on the strip written by sociologists and other scholars. I saw an elitist bias at the basis of this situation and asked a question in my book that has continued to interest me: "why is popular culture so unpopular?" Comics were useful, critics suggested at the time, only for one reason—to wrap garbage. I am exaggerating things a bit here, but in essence that was the case. I argued, to the contrary, that in many respects there were no essential differences between popular culture and "elite" culture—a position that was radical at the time but which, in our post-modern world, has become a generally accepted notion—at least by post-modern critics.

Even some sociologists believed that popular culture was irrelevant. One sociologist, Melvin Tumin, who was teaching at Princeton, told me at a conference (in the early seventies) that he devoted half an hour to popular culture in one of his seminars. That was, he said, more than enough time to deal with it. Things have changed considerably since then, and with the recent development of cultural studies, we now find everyone, from professors of literature to sociologists to communications scholars to philosophers dealing with the mass media and popular culture.

Around the time that *Li'l Abner*, the first book to be written on a comic strip, was published, there suddenly appeared a number of general books on the comics—many of which were profusely illustrated. In 1967, George Perry and Alan Aldridge published *The Penguin Book of Comics*, which dealt mainly with British and American comics. It was, as the authors described it, "a slight history."

A year later, in 1968, Pierre Couperie and Maurice Horn's *A*

History of the Comic Strip was published. It was originally a French publication with a much more serious title for the French edition, which would be translated as "Comic Strips and Narrative Figuration." It was written in conjunction with an exhibition of comic strip art at The Louvre. In 1971 Les Daniels put out *Comix: A History of Comic Books in America.* Then, in 1972, Reinhold Reitberger and Wolfgang Fuchs published *Comics: Anatomy of a Mass Medium,* which was a translation of a German book published the year before. It was a much more substantial book than the Penguin book.

My interest in the comics led to the publication of *The Comic-Stripped American* in 1974. In this book I took a number of the most important comic strips and comic books and analyzed them in terms of what they reflected about American society and culture. In the book I made extensive use of psychoanalytic theory and semiotic theory, though, at the time, I didn't think of myself as a semiotician. The book was published by Walker & Co., and it was later picked up by Penguin books as a paperback.

A huge book edited by Maurice Horn, *The World Encyclopedia of Comics,* came out in 1976. The book is a large format one and is approximately eight hundred pages of double-columned text. It is probably the most important reference book for those interested in the comics and contains an excellent citation on Al Capp written by Bill Blackbeard, perhaps the dean of comic strip scholars in the United States, that covers everything from the start of Capp's career, at age nineteen, drawing *Col. Gilfeather* to the accusations that appeared about his seducing college girls. The book also contains a citation on *Li'l Abner* itself, also written by Blackbeard.

In recent years there have been a number of scholarly books on the comics. UNESCO published a book, *Comics and Visual Culture: Research Studies from Ten Countries,* that deals with comics in such countries as France, Kenya, Japan, India, Italy, and the Soviet Union. The title of the book suggests a different way of looking at comics: they are part of visual culture and pose interesting questions for those who do research on subjects such as perception and cognition.

Judith O'Sullivan published *The Great American Comic Strip: One Hundred Years of Cartoon Art* in 1990 (she had earlier prepared a catalogue for an exhibition of comics called *The Art of the Comic Strip* at the University of Maryland Art Gallery). Also in 1990, M. Thomas Inge published *Comics as Culture*. This collection of scholarly essays (many of which had appeared previously in journals and books) on comics and cartoons puts the issue of the relation between the comics and culture on the front burner:

> . . . comic strips and comic books reflect larger cultural trends. Relations between literature, technology, art, and the comics are explored in general chapters and discussions of specific major artists. But the comics are not important because of these connections. My intent is to suggest ways the comics also deal with the larger aesthetic and philosophic issues mainstream culture has always defined in its arts and humanities. The comics are another form of legitimate culture quite capable of confronting the major questions of mankind, but they do it with a gentler spirit that leads to laughter at the moment of recognition. (xxi)

All of these books suggest a new sensibility relative to popular culture, in general, and the comics, in particular. The comics, it has been suggested, are an American idiom. Comics may be a "naive" art form, but this naivete only increases their ability to communicate with ordinary people and their value as a means of getting at popular taste, beliefs, and values, for the researcher.

In addition to these surveys and scholarly books, there are now many collections of comics—and a number of our classic comic strips, such as *Peanuts, Little Orphan Annie*, and *Li'l Abner* are now available in substantial reprint volumes. These collections furnish an invaluable source for culture critics, for unlike other media, such as film and television, the comic strip sits on the page, and thus is much easier to deal with than works found in electronic media. And our comic strips furnish a record that goes back, in some cases, fifty or more years. Even though there are a number of books on the comics, if you think about their importance, it would seem that they still are not being given the attention they deserve.

It is an interesting experience to read a book one wrote thirty years earlier. In preparing to write this afterword, I also read some of my journals from the early sixties, when I was in graduate school and Italy, and thinking about comics and popular culture. How does one explain a choice? I'm not sure why I decided to write on *Li'l Abner*. Yes, I was interested in humor, but why a comic strip and not, say, political humor—which one of my favorite professors, David Noble, had suggested I consider? And once I had decided to write on the comics, why *Li'l Abner* and not *Krazy Kat* or some other strip?

One reason I chose *Li'l Abner* was that I really loved the strip. At times Capp was absolutely brilliant, and I can recall when I was reading the strip at United Features how I would actually start laughing hysterically at one of Capp's gags. The people at United Features probably thought I was crazy. Capp was Jewish, and maybe I responded to a certain Jewish quality in his humor. I was an artist, of sorts, and had taken courses with Ian MacIver at the University of Massachusetts and Jim Lechay at the University of Iowa. I learned how to draw caricatures and used to make money doing them. Could my work as a cartoonist and caricaturist somehow have influenced me?

Whatever the case, when I decided to write about *Li'l Abner*, I found that I also had to write about popular culture in general. In a sense, my dissertation forced me to open a door—to the analysis of popular culture of every nature, from comics to television programs—and when I walked through that door I had, without knowing it at the time, found my life's work. I had planted a seed that was to grow into my career.

Publishing a book is always exciting. You ask yourself questions such as "what impact will my book have on the subject?" and "how will it be received?" and "will it affect my career?" But being asked to write an afterword for a second printing (a kind of second coming) of a book thirty years later is infinitely more exciting. For one thing, it suggests that someone—in this case Tom Inge and editor Seetha A-Srinivasan at the University Press of Mississippi—feel that the book is worth putting out again and still has something to say to people. And that is a wonderful feeling. I am grateful for this "vote of confidence."

I hope my readers will find the second appearance of *Li'l Abner* to be of some value, for methodological as well as historical reasons, and that they will come away from the book with the feeling that maybe they would like to open and step through the same door I stepped through thirty years ago.

Appendix

Although the serious study of comic strips is only beginning now in America, there is considerable interest in this form in Italy and, so I have been told, in Europe. In the January 12, 1965 issue of *Il Mondo*, an important Italian weekly that deals with politics, culture, and society, there was an article by Cesare Mannucci entitled "Sociologia del fumetto"—"The Sociology of the Comic Strip," as we would put it.

In this article, Mr. Manucci mentioned that the University of Rome has recently started archives on the comics, and that in conjunction with these archives, a society has been founded for the systematic study of comics. There is already in existence in Milan a similar "Comics Club," led by Umberto Eco and a group of Milanese intellectuals, whose interests also include popular culture items such as hit songs and television programs. Eco, who is Professor of Mass Communications at the University of Turino, has written a remarkable study—*Apocalittici e Integrati*—dealing with how comic strips should be analyzed, both as an art form and as socially and politically interesting documents.

Roberto Giammanco, an Italian social scientist whose *Dialago sulla societa americana*[1] has a great deal to say about American comics, has recently completed a long study of "Li'l Abner" and other American comics called *Gulp*. Also, the first international symposium on the comics was held in Italy in the winter of 1965, which signified the recognition, by European scholars, of the possibilities in the comics. This event is held annually.

To give some idea of the nature of this interest, let me conclude by quoting from Mannucci's article:

> . . . we don't consider the comics, as in years past, as reading for underdeveloped intelligences, for children or for the ignorant. Now the comic strip, which illuminates its culture, is seen as important material.

He adds:

> Today it is not enough to extend sociological and psychological research to the comics and the photo-romances of the forties and fifties, that is, to the literature that has nourished large strata of the ordinary people after the war, in order to be able to better understand the way they act. This has now come to be considered routine (even, if up to now, there has been little of it).
> . . . There is instead a vast and enthusiastic work of unwinding the past, a work of the most elevated order and of the most arduous nature . . . research on the most intimate sources of culture, on the ideology and psychology of the last forty years.[2]

It is quite evident that in Italy the study of the comics is now looked upon as a most important field of inquiry, and one worthy of serious and extended attention.

Notes and References

INTRODUCTION

1. My use of the term "comics" is explained in this study. In America we use the term to cover material that is quite obviously not humorous.

2. For the sake of clarity, I refer to the strip as "Li'l Abner" and the character as Abner.

3. I use a number of techniques (such as textual analysis and literary history) from different disciplines in dealing with the various aspects of "Li'l Abner." For a more complete discussion of my methods, see the conclusion.

4. I have read about a third of the strip for this study. Since there are about ten or fifteen different episodes a year (a typical one lasts five weeks), I have only been able to use a small percentage of Capp's work in my analysis. However, in choosing what I consider to be his most representative work, covering a large number of years, I feel I have been able to do justice to him.

5. Al Capp, *From Dogpatch to Slobbovia,* ed. D. M. White (Boston, 1964), unpaged.

6. *Ibid.*

7. John Cawelti, "Prolegomena to the Western," *Studies in Public Communication,* IV (Autumn, 1962), 58.

Notes & References

1. I shall use such terms as "mass" culture, "popular" culture, and "popular art" interchangeably.

2. The very fact that I can be so cavalier about culture shows how democratic the times are. There seems to be no definition of culture, *per se*, that everyone accepts—and I am not going to define it because my concern is with popular culture. What popular culture is will be discussed in some detail in this chapter. I might add that there is little agreement on what *satire* is, on what the *grotesque* is, and on any number of subjects that I will be discussing. I shall not attempt to offer definitions of these controversial subjects but shall assume that there is some kind of "understanding" that I can build upon. I shall also bring to bear important scholarship in these areas so that there will be a number of distinctions made even if I am not able to offer conclusive definitions.

3. Glencoe, Ill., 1957, p. v.

4. See *Daedalus*, Spring, 1960 issue on "Mass Culture and Mass Media."

5. "Mass Culture and Social Criticism," *Daedalus* (Spring, 1960), p. 388.

6. See Robert Giammanco's *Dialogo sulla societa americana* (Turin, 1964).

7. *Principles of Literary Criticism* (London, 1924), p. 203.

8. For studies on these subjects see: M. Wolfenstein and N. Leites, *Movies: A Psychological Study*; Charles A. Siepmann, *Radio, Television and Society*; James D. Hart, *The Popular Book*; D. M. White and H. Abel, *The Funnies: An American Idiom*.

9. There are some fifty articles, of varying lengths, which discuss or mention "Li'l Abner" in the period 1934-1964. Most of these articles tend to be short news items that have appeared in *Time, Life,* and *Newsweek*, and are not critically interesting. I shall use all relevant articles in the course of the study, rather than include a special section on them.

10. In an effort to make it possible for the reader to examine many of the comics discussed in this chapter, I have, as much as possible, analyzed characters and adventures found in *I Primi Eroi* of Garzanti and *La Corriere dei Piccoli*, though I have consulted and used other publications.

11. The Italian term for what we call comics.

12. Few of the "classic" Italian comics (such as "Bonventura," "Bilbolbul," "Pier Cloruro," or "Pampurio") have the highly stylized, toothpick limbs and big feet that are found in "Beetle Bailey" or in Disney characters, such as Mickey Mouse. Both this kind of stylization

and exaggeration and the realistic, "draftsman" type comic strip (which is not usually comic) are more or less American innovations, and fairly recent ones at that. "Mickey Mouse" dates from 1928; "draftsman" style comics from Milton Caniff's "Terry and the Pirates," 1934.

13. This information was obtained in an interview with the editor of the Mickey Mouse comics in Italy.

14. One might almost say that American individualism tends to be economic and political, whereas Italian individualism is social. The American is a friendly fellow who "conforms," invites you to dinner at the drop of a hat, but believes in free enterprise and classical economics. The Italian (and European) lives in a much more closed society, where people are more self-directed, but politically he has much more of a sense of the group—at least this is suggested by the existence of various Socialist parties in Italy.

15. The code was drawn up to prevent government intervention.

16. "Li'l Abner," June 9, 1960.

17. Al Capp, *The World of Li'l Abner* (New York, 1956), p. 74.

CHAPTER TWO

1. *Anatomy of Criticism* (Princeton, N.J., 1957), p. 224.

2. *The Anatomy of Satire* (Princeton, N.J., 1962), p. 206.

3. *Ibid.*, p. 208.

4. Frye, p. 224.

5. *Caricature* (London, 1957), p. 11.

6. *Swift and the Satirist's Art* (Chicago, 1963), p. 31.

7. Hoffman's study of caricature and Rosenheim's study of satire are both recommended as being valuable sources of information on two controversial subjects. It should be noted that "Li'l Abner" fits Rosenheim's definition as well as most others.

8. "Li'l Abner" made its first appearance on Monday, August 13, 1934, in seven newspapers. In 1960 it was appearing regularly in nearly nine hundred daily and Sunday newspapers in America and almost one hundred foreign newspapers in twenty-eight countries. An estimated fifty or sixty million people now follow the strip daily.

9. Dogpatch was originally located in Kentucky, but as the strip progressed, the location became more and more indefinite.

10. The Yokum family has been a matriarchy right from the beginning of the strip. The size of Mammy and Pappy has fluctuated, but the authority has always been firmly seated in Mammy.

11. Capp, *The World of Li'l Abner*, n.p.

12. Bergson sees the use of types as necessary in comedy. See his essay "Laughter."

13. "The Meanings of Comedy" in *Comedy* (New York, 1956), p. 219.

14. *Ibid.,* p. 201.

15. Comedy has generally been seen as social and tragedy as more concerned with the fate of individuals.

16. New York, 1959, unpaged.

17. *A Secret History of the Line,* in *American Poetry and Prose,* ed. Norman Foerster (Boston, Mass., 1957), I, 106.

18. *Ibid.,* p. 107.

19. In *An Anthology of American Humor,* ed. Brom Weber (New York, 1962), p. 266.

20. Capp, *From Dogpatch to Slobbovia.*

21. Weber, p. 249.

22. *Ibid.*

23. Capp, *World of Li'l Abner.*

24. There is a considerable amount of debate on the origin, function, and importance of myth, as well as its definition. Stanley Edgar Hyman has a long discussion of this subject in his book *The Promised End.* He obviously sides with the Cambridge school, which sees myth as arising out of ritual—as "the spoken correlative of the acted rite," as Jane Harrison puts it. Opposed to this theory is the "psychoanalytical school," which, Hoffman says, claims "all myths are one myth, and that the mythic levels of consciousness as found in primitive people correspond to the infantile or neurotic consciousness of modern man." Hoffman finds neither theory adequate but both useful. His discussion of romance, folklore, and myth is recommended.

25. New York, 1961, p. xiii.

26. *Mark Twain and Southwestern Humor* (Boston, 1959), p. 62.

27. *Ibid.,* p. 61.

28. *Ibid.,* p. 64.

29. London, 1937, p. 127.

30. Capp, *From Dogpatch to Slobbovia.*

31. Weber, p. 266.

32. See *Rogue's Progress: Studies in the Picaresque Novel* (Cambridge, 1964).

33. *The Grotesque: An American Genre and other Essays* (Carbondale, Illinois, 1962), p. 4.

34. *Ibid.,* p. 8.

35. *Ibid.,* p. 19.

36. Quoted by O'Connor, p. 5.

37. *The Art of Satire* (Cambridge, Mass., 1940), p. 70.

38. *Ibid.,* p. 68.

39. Frye, p. 186.

40. See Richard Chase, *The American Novel and Its Tradition* (New York, 1957), for a discussion of this subject.

41. *A Treasury of Jewish Humor* (New York, 1951), p. 734.

42. There is a controversy that rages between Capp and Fisher over the matter of using hillbillies in the comics. Fisher claims Capp stole the idea of using hillbillies from him. However, there were hillbillies in American comics in the early 1900's, in George Luke's work. See *Newsweek* (November 29, 1948) for a discussion of this matter.

CHAPTER THREE

1. The most thorough discussion of specific subjects, such as the businessman, the politician, law, etc., has been reserved for the chapters on Capp's dialogue and art style, and the conclusion.

2. This will be discussed in some detail in the chapter on Capp's dialogue.

3. Frye, p. 172.

4. *A Glossary of Literary Terms* (New York, 1961), p. 89.

5. Worcester, p. 14. Also see Freud, *Jokes and Their Relation to the Unconscious.*

6. Orrin E. Klapp, *Heroes, Villains, and Fools* (Englewood Cliffs, N.J., 1962), p. 163.

7. *Ibid.*

8. Sypher, p. 232.

9. *Ibid.*, p. 233.

10. *Ibid.*, p. 234.

11. Highet, p. 206.

12. *Ibid.*, p. 208.

13. According to Moses Hadas, slapstick itself is intellectual. He divides comedy into two parts: sentimental, which appeals to the heart, and intellectual, which appeals to the head. See his introduction to *The Complete Plays of Aristophanes* (New York, 1962), pp. 1-8.

14. Al Capp, "The Comedy of Charlie Chaplin" in *The Funnies*, ed. D. M. White and R. H. Abel (New York, 1963), pp. 265, 266.

15. Edmund Bergler, *Laughter and the Sense of Humor* (New York, 1956), p. 4.

16. Capp, "Chaplin," p. 268.

17. *Ibid.*, p. 265. This is Capp's theory; I would disagree.

18. *Ibid.*, p. 266.

19. Sylvan Barnet, *et al.*, *A Dictionary of Literary Terms* (Boston, 1960), p. 19.

20. This subject is discussed in more detail in the conclusion.

21. "Male and Female Relations in the American Comic Strip" in White and Abel, *The Funnies*, p. 231.

22. "How To Read Li'l Abner Intelligently," in *Mass Culture*, eds. Bernard Rosenberg and David Manning White (Glencoe, Ill., 1957), p. 218.

23. "Li'l Abner," December 13, 1964.

CHAPTER FOUR

1. I am using the term "dialogue" to mean all language in the strip, not just conversations.

2. See *Newsweek* (November 24, 1947) for a discussion of this matter.

3. "Expressiveness and Symbolism" in *A Book of Esthetics*, ed. M. Rader (New York, 1960), p. 254.

4. Capp, *The World of Li'l Abner*, p. 791.

5. See Frye, pp. 226-228 for a discussion of this subject. Also, Sypher, pp. 228-230.

6. Capp, *The World of Li'l Abner*, p. 92.

7. *Ibid.*, p. 175.

8. Melbourne, 1951, p. 66.

9. *The Random House Dictionary* (unabridged edition) defines wit as "the keen perception and cleverly apt expression of those connections between ideas which awaken amusement and pleasure."

10. "Li'l Abner," May 23, 1960.

11. See the Foreword by Jerry Capp in Capp, *The Return of the Shmoo*, pp. 3, 4.

12. *Ibid.* (after introduction).

13. *The Random House Dictionary* (unabridged edition) defines "Schmo" as "a foolish, boring, or stupid person; a jerk" and ties it to the Yiddish form *Schmok*, "fool."

14. Capp, *The Return of the Shmoo*.

15. Capp, *The Life and Times of the Shmoo*, pp. 76, 77.

16. It has also been seen as a female "womb-symbol"—representing Mother Earth, but this does not seem to explain everything. Capp tells us that the earth is a Shmoo at the conclusion of the episode.

17. Capp, *The Return of the Shmoo*.

18. "Talk of the Town," *New Yorker* (October 26, 1963), p. 40.

19. *Ibid.*

20. *Native American Humor* (San Francisco, 1960), p. 121.

21. Like his brother Abner, Tiny Yokum also functions as the servant (and protector—as bodyguard, for instance) of the rich and powerful.

22. The following dialogue took place in "Li'l Abner" during the period May 30 to June 30, 1960. Capp is obviously capitalizing on the so-called "Abominable Snow Man" who keeps popping up in newspapers.

23. Capp, *From Dogpatch to Slobbovia*.

24. Capp, "Li'l Abner," November, 1964.

25. C. A. Robinson, Jr., ed. *An Anthology of Greek Drama* (New York, 1950), p. 228.

26. New York, 1956, p. 307.

27. I have used E. S. Bates' literary adaptation of the Bible for my source, p. 274. This version does not have the traditional chapter and verse organization found in most Bibles; in conventionally arranged Bibles, the passage will be found at II Sam. 3:33-34.

28. New York, 1960, p. 176.

29. For a discussion of what is behind personal and family names, see Mario Pei's *The Story of Language*.

30. The term "dick" also happens to be a slang expression for "penis." This would indicate, to continue our analysis of Capp's phallicism, that Fosdick, i.e., "fearless" masculine sexuality, must be abused by society. I admit this is a bit far-fetched.

CHAPTER FIVE

1. See White and Abel, *The Funnies*.

2. Wolfgang Kayser makes a distinction between the grotesque and caricature in his book *The Grotesque In Art and Literature*. He sees the grotesque as a somewhat intensified caricature that attacks the very order of existence.

3. *Webster's New Collegiate Dictionary*.

4. See Ernst Kris, *Psychoanalytic Explorations in Art* (New York, 1952), p. 197.

5. *Ibid.*, p. 180.

6. See Sigmund Freud's tenth lecture "Symbolism in Dreams" in *A General Introduction to Psychoanalysis*.

7. See "Li'l Abner," July, 1960.

8. Kris, p. 215.

9. London, 1928, p. 32.

10. In *I Fumetti*, Carlo della Corte links Capp to New Deal liberalism and others have seen Capp as championing liberal causes—civil rights, free enterprise, etc. As Capp mentioned in his *New Yorker* interview, he has been attacked because his Shmoos were interpreted by many as socialistic and an attack on capitalism. He has also been praised for his stand against foreign aid, a subject upon which liberals are split. Defining liberalism is a very difficult task. Schlesinger has a section on it in *The Politics of Hope* which is so vague as to be almost useless. In recent years there seems to have been a change in Capp's political orientation and he is much more conservative now.

CHAPTER SIX

1. Klapp, p. 163. He continues: "As an example I would cite the

remarkable amount of social criticism to be found in one episode from Al Capp's 'Li'l Abner.' The hero is shown in a Quixotic role, that is, a person with a heart of gold getting into trouble by helping others. Abner answers an advertisement by a clothing company for the man with the lowest I.Q. in the world. The job is to risk his neck publicizing zootsuits at a salary of eight dollars a week. (The theory is that the public will be so captivated by such a hero that they will rush to wear whatever he wears.) Clad in a preposterous zootsuit with floppy tie and padded shoulders (his armor?) he undertakes missions to help anyone who calls In one case, he climbs a tree to rescue a kitten for a lady, but at the top finds a wildcat and falls, all bitten and torn, while the crowd cheers. His exploits finally make him so popular that he is nominated for President of the United States by the 'Zoot Suit Progressive Party.' —Thus, in one episode, Capp strikes at a number of American values themes: (1) the healthy American boy (naive enough to be taken advantage of); (2) the ideal of the do-gooder ('Eight dollars a week!!—Oh (sob!), thank you gennulmen!—But, honestly—it hain't th' big money which attracks me—it's the chance t' do *good*!!'); (3) judgment of popular majorities (captivated by such a hero); (4) a current political viewpoint; (5) a clothing fashion; and (6) by implication the tone of a society that could provide a scene for such activities."

2. Robert Brustein, "The Anti-Establishmentarians," *The New Republic* (February 23, 1963), p. 28, G. William Domhoff argues to the contrary in *Who Rules America?* and is quite persuasive.

3. Boston, 1963, p. 227.

4. Interview in *The New Yorker* (October 26, 1963), p. 40.

5. This charge is often made against Twain.

6. *The Satirist, His Temperament, Motivation, and Influence* (Ames, Iowa, 1963), p. 253.

7. *Daumier, Caricaturist* (Emmaus, Penna. 1954), p. 1.

8. "Li'l Abner," week of December 14, 1955.

9. For example, America is a country that is identified with both Pragmatism and Natural Law.

10. Gilbert Chase, *America's Music* (New York, 1955), p. 22.

11. Boston, 1967, p. 64.

APPENDIX

1. For a review of this book, see my article in *Il Mulino*, Bologna, May, 1964.

2. Translation by A. Berger.

Selected Bibliography

BOOKS

ALTER, ROBERT. *Rogue's Progress: Study in the Picaresque Novel.* Cambridge, Mass.: Harvard University Press, 1964. Study of the nature of the picaresque hero and his role based upon historical study and literary analysis, sees the picaresque hero as unconcerned with morality yet having a moral function by being a touchstone and putting men to the test, so to speak. This book is Alter's Ph.D. thesis in comparative literature at Harvard.

ASHBEE, C. R. *Caricature.* London: Chapman and Hall, 1928. History of caricature and analysis of the various aspects of the art and its social function: says that caricature offers the whole story of the Reformation and religious wars of Europe, though in a rather savage manner; defines caricature as "grotesque or ludicrous representation of persons or things by exaggeration of their most characteristic feature," yet recognizes that this definition is inadequate.

AUSUBEL, NATHAN (ed.). *A Treasury of Jewish Humor.* New York: Doubleday, 1951. Collection of stories and jokes about typically Jewish types (Paskudniks and No-Goodniks, Chuspaniks, Shmendriks and Shmiggeges, etc.) and other Jewish subjects; short preface on Jewish humor and glossary that explains certain terms.

Selected Bibliography

BECKER, STEPHEN (ed.). *Comic Art in America*. New York: Simon and Schuster, 1959. Social history of the funnies, political cartoons, magazine humor, and animated cartoons; valuable source of cartoons and comics but little analysis, almost four hundred illustrations and a considerable amount of factual material, dates, etc.

BERGLER, EDMUND. *Laughter and the Sense of Humor*. New York: Intercontinental Medical Book Company, 1956. Psychoanalytical analysis of humor, sees it as a means of warding off internal fears and the inner conscience: ". . . all forms of wit, humor and the comic are *directed at one specific inner danger: the accusation by inner conscience that one is a lover of the pleasure-in-displeasure pattern —psychic masochism.*" Valuable analysis of some eighty theories of humor.

BLAIR, WALTER. *Native American Humor*. San Francisco: Chandler Publishing Co., 1960. One of the most influential books on American humor: has a long introduction discussing what is "American" in American humor, and the various periods in American humor from 1775 to the present day; also has a thirteen-page bibliography of articles and books on American humor, as well as good sampling of American humor from "Down East" to Twain.

BOATRIGHT, MODY C. *Folk Laughter on the American Frontier*. New York: Collier Books, 1961. Discussion of development of folk humor in America; excellent bibliographies and numerous examples of folk humor.

CAPP, AL. *The Life and Times of the Shmoo*. New York: Simon and Schuster, 1948. Collection of "Li'l Abner" strips which dealt with the adventures of the Shmoo; has a fantastic appendix which supposedly explains something about life in Dogpatch. More than seven hundred-thousand copies of this book were sold.
——. *The Return of the Shmoo*. New York: Simon and Schuster, 1959. More adventures of the Shmoo when brought back in "Li'l Abner" some ten years after it first appeared.
——. *The World of Li'l Abner*. New York: Ballantine Books, 1953. Collection of various episodes covering a number of years of the strip, with different adventures that appeared in 1946-1951. Introduction by John Steinbeck (which claims that Capp is "the best writer in America"), foreword by Charles Chaplin (which praises Capp for his inventiveness and talent). Capp also has a short introduction in which he explains his "formula." Later editions of the book do not include the Chaplin foreword.

CARADEC, FR. and staff of Garzanti publishers. *I Primi Eroi*. Milan:

Garzanti Publishers, 1962. Encyclopedic work containing hundreds of different comic strips from many different countries. No analysis, though there is a short historical study of the development of comic strips through the ages. A major source for anyone interested in comparing popular culture (comparative "sub-literature") as seen in children's comics. The only drawback is that it is only printed in Italian and no English edition is anticipated.

DELLA CORTE, CARLO. *I. Fumetti. Milan:* Mondadori, 1961. Social and psychological study of what we call "comic strips," deals in some detail with numerous American strips. A popular study—part of Mondadori's "Popular Encyclopedia" series—but useful. Much of the book devoted to American comics, also has a valuable short bibliography showing which European scholars have written on the comics.

FEINBERG, LIONEL. *The Satirist: His Temperament, Motivation, and Influence.* Ames, Iowa: Iowa State University Press, 1963. Attempt to reach an understanding of satire by focusing upon the satirist, his personality, etc.; sees the satirist as an "attacker" and satire as a *"playfully critical distortion of the familiar,"* says there is no logical place (i.e., radical or conservative) in which we should except to find satirists, as their political position depends upon their beliefs and their temperaments, and few satirists have enough courage to attack the basic elements of the social, economic, or political makeup of their country.

FREUD, SIGMUND. *Jokes and Their Relation to the Unconscious,* ed. and trans. JAMES STRACHEY. New York: W. W. Norton, 1960. This classic psychological analysis of wit and humor, which first appeared in 1905 in Vienna, concludes with a formula: "The pleasure in jokes has seemed to us to arise from an economy in expenditure upon inhibition, the pleasure in the comic from an economy in expenditure upon ideation (upon cathexis) and the pleasure in humour from an economy in expenditure upon feeling. In all three modes of working of our mental apparatus the pleasure is derived from an economy." Has also been translated as *Wit and Its Relation to the Unconscious.*

FRYE, NORTHROP. *Anatomy of Criticism.* Princeton, N.J.: Princeton University Press, 1957. Four essays on historical, ethical, archetypal, and rhetorical criticism which form part of a rather elaborate system of classes and subclasses for placing literature and analyzing it. I was most interested in Frye's comments on satire and humor. The work is, as I understand it, controversial.

Selected Bibliography

GROTJAHN, MARTIN. *Beyond Laughter*. New York: McGraw-Hill, 1957. Freudian analysis of wit and humor that has some interesting things to say about Little Moron jokes, Kilroy was here, Ferdinand the Bull, and Mickey Mouse. Grotjahn is concerned with the way humor is used to ward off or disguise guilt feelings and fear of castration. Good bibliography of psychoanalytical material on humor.

GURKO, LEO. *Heroes, Highbrows and the Popular Mind*. New York: Bobbs-Merrill, 1953. Discussion of popular culture and society which says "our mass media reflect with special accuracy many of the convictions of our intensely middle-class nation: its acquisitiveness and sentimentality, its queer mixture of high-mindedness and cynicism." Sees American thought as pervaded with paradoxes, such as the idea that wealth corrupts existing side by side with the worship of material success.

HADAS, MOSES (ed.). *The Complete Plays of Aristophanes*. New York: Bantam Books, 1968. The introduction discusses satire and comedy in terms of both their formal qualities and their social and political implications. Hadas mentions that when the tyrant of Syracuse wanted to know what the Athenians were really like, Plato told him to read the comedies of Aristophanes, and suggests that comedy is a valuable source of information on what we call "national character."

HIGHET, GILBERT. *The Anatomy of Satire*. Princeton, N.J.: Princeton University Press, 1962. Analysis of what satire is and how it is generally used; discusses the structure of satire, the motives of the satirist, and the functions of satire, and makes a number of distinctions concerning such devices as farce, hoax, parody, etc. Sees satire as "protreptic"; satirists "give positive advice. They set up an exemplar to copy. They state an ideal."

HOFFMAN, WERNER. *Caricature from Leonardo to Picasso*. London: John Calder, 1957. Discussion of the historical development of caricature, the artistic impulses necessary for it (observation of reality objectively and transformation of it subjectively), and the social and philosophic meaning of the form. Mentions how difficult it is to make a distinction between caricature and the grotesque. Sees a continuum of sorts, with caricature as closer "to the real world which it can't lose sight of." Defines caricature as "all representations in which the appearance of human beings is consciously exaggerated or their physiognomy intensified, irrespective of whether it is a portrait, the invention of a type or an indiscreet extract from the world of everyday things." Also a good discussion of political caricature in the book, which says that its very success has lessened its impact.

JAMES, HENRY. *Daumier, Caricaturist.* Emmaus, Penna.: Emmaus, 1954. Short discussion of the nature of caricature and the work of Daumier. Sees caricature as a pictorial form of journalistic satire, speculates upon why caricature hasn't achieved a "high destiny" in America and concludes that it is because America is too young to be able to be critical about itself and to accept its incongruities.

KAYSER, WOLFGANG. *The Grotesque: In Art and Literature,* trans. U. WEISSTEIN. Bloomington, Indiana: Indiana University Press, 1963. After an analysis of the term "grotesque" and of a number of examples of the grotesque taken from both art and literature, concludes that the grotesque is "an attempt to invoke and subdue the demonic aspects of the world." This definition doesn't really do justice to Kayser's analysis, which sees the grotesque as an attack on the very order of the world, as involving "an inhuman, nocturnal, and abysmal realm." Sees the grotesque as something different from the comic (where, I think, we would put caricature) and much closer to the monstrous.

KLAPP, ORRIN E. *Heroes, Villains, and Fools: The Changing American Character.* Englewood Cliffs, N.J.: Prentice-Hall, 1962. Surveys "the major social types of American society which serve prominently as its models." Sees the three basic types as heroes, villains, and fools and breaks each of these types into numerous subtypes; sees a deterioration in American character.

KRIS, ERNST. *Psychoanalytic Explorations in Art.* New York: International Universities Press, 1952. A collection of articles which seems to have the status of being a classic in its field, examines a number of aspects of art from a psychoanalytical point of view. Sections on creativity, the art of the insane, problems of literary criticism, and the comic (and caricature). Many of the essays were written in collaboration with specialists in art history, aesthetics, etc. I used it for its long discussion of the psychology and principles of caricature. Profusely illustrated, has a long, twenty-two-page bibliography. Now out in paperback.

LIPSET, SEYMOUR MARTIN. *The First New Nation: The United States in Historical and Comparative Perspective.* New York: Basic Books, 1963. Study of American history and society documents author's contention that equality and achievement have been, and still are, basic American values and that American character has not been changed greatly by industrialization and urbanization, as Reisman and Whyte suggest. Excellent bibliographical references in its numerous footnotes.

LYNN, KENNETH S. *Mark Twain and Southwestern Humor*. Boston: Atlantic/Little, Brown, 1959. Valuable discussion of the development and nature of Southwestern humor and the humor of Twain which stresses political considerations. Sees Twain's revolt against the Republican party as leading to a "wholesale contempt" for American's business civilization."

MCLUHAN, HERBERT MARSHALL. *The Mechanical Bride: Folklore of Industrial Man*. New York: Vanguard, 1951. In this rather unusual book, which is a commentary that attempts to "release some of the meaning" found in what McLuhan postulates as the new folklore: advertisements, detective stories, comic strips, etc., the reader finds short explanations and evaluations of the concepts behind this material. There is no continuity to the book (it can be read in any order the reader wishes) but it does have a number of thought-provoking and perceptive things to say about contemporary society, its values, its goals, and its problems. McLuhan has a wide-ranging erudition and makes a number of interesting connections (such as seeing the picnic as a modern, utopian version of the pastoral) in this rather free-swinging book.

MUNRO, D. H. *Argument of Laughter*. Melbourne, Australia: Melbourne University Press, 1951. Divides humor into ten classes and discusses each class, concluding that it involves some kind of incongruity. Munro believes that stereotypes actually influence our judgments of real people.

MURRELL, WILLIAM. *A History of American Graphic Humor*. 2 vols. New York: Macmillan, 1938. Illustrated history of American graphic humor from Revolutionary War days to pre-World War II days; concludes that there is something particularly American about our graphic humor, a "peculiar graphic vernacular and accent" tied to American politics, customs, and prejudices.

O'CONNOR, WILLIAM VAN. *The Grotesque: An American Genre*. Carbondale, Ill.: Southern Illinois University Press. 1962. Valuable discussion of the grotesque in American literature and a number of other subjects related to American life and literature.

ROSENBERG, BERNARD and DAVID MANNING WHITE (eds.). *Mass Culture: The Popular Arts in America*. Glencoe, Ill.: Free Press, 1957. Probably the most influential collection of articles on the various aspects of mass culture available; sections on the comics, radio and television, advertising, the movies, etc. and theoretical considerations.

ROSENHEIM, EDWARD W. *Swift and the Satirist's Art.* Chicago: University of Chicago Press, 1963. A recent contribution to the study of satire, asserts that there are two basic kinds of satire—punitive and persuasive—and offers a definition of satire, "an attack by means of a manifest fiction upon discernible historical particulars." This definition has, in turn, been attacked as being too narrow. Attempts to distinguish between comedy and satire, and reminds us that many works aren't completely satirical but contain satirical elements.

ROURKE, CONSTANCE. *American Humor: A Study of the National Character.* New York: Harcourt, Brace, 1931. One of the first studies of American humor; examines certain American types (such as the Yankee, the Negro Minstrel, etc.) and relates them to American life and literature. Miss Rourke was one of the first to recognize the importance of Henry James. She sees American Humor starting in the 1830's—a debatable matter, since others see it starting with the Revolutionary War and others with the Puritans.

SCHLESINGER, ARTHUR M., JR. *The Politics of Hope, Boston:* Houghton Mifflin, 1963. Collection of articles on a number of contemporary public issues: discusses, in a rather broad manner, the conflict between liberals and conservatives, has articles on Walter Lippmann, Reinhold Niebuhr, Whittaker Chambers, etc., and a section entitled "Politics and Culture" on popular culture.

SHERIDAN, MARTIN. *Comics and Their Creators: Life Stories of American Cartoonists.* Boston: Hale, Cushman and Flint, 1944. Essentially an annotated list of comic strip artists, with a short introduction on the history of the comics in America and a great deal of illustrative material; very little analytical material.

SYPHER, WYLIE (ed.). *Comedy.* New York: Archer Books, 1956. Contains two articles on humor—one by Bergson and one by Meredith—and a valuable introduction and appendix on the subject by Sypher. The appendix, entitled "The Meanings of Comedy," is an important analysis of the structure of comedy, its historical background, and its social meaning. Sees comedy as keeping us pure by forcing us to look at ourselves skeptically.

WARNER, W. LLOYD. *American Life: Dream and Reality.* Chicago: University of Chicago Press, 1953. Important study of various aspects of American society, such as voluntary associations, the importance of the family, social class and color caste, social mobility and the mass media. Shows how soap operas strengthen and stabilize the American social structure by reinforcing the housewife's sense of the importance of her role. Has a good deal on the various social classes and their roles in American society.

WHITE, D. M. and H. H. ABEL, (eds.)*The Funnies: An American Idiom.* New York: Free Press, 1963. Anthology dealing with various aspects of the comic strip. The first scholarly work devoted exclusively to comics, has an extensive bibliography.

ARTICLES

Note: Although there have been a large number of articles on Capp and "Li'l Abner" in the periodical press, most of them have been news items (such as the most recent one, in the February 22, 1965 issue of *Newsweek* announcing that a soft drink called "Kickapoo Joy Juice" will be marketed with Capp's blessings). Few of the articles have been analytical.

On Capp

Arthur Brodbeck and David M. White, "How to Read Li'l Abner Intelligently," published for the first time in *Mass Culture*. Discussion of Mammy Yokum as the overprotecting mother, sees the strip as essentially realistic and accurate depiction of "the unconscious and unrecognized forces at work in American life." This article was one of the first to understand complex nature of Capp's artistry.

E. J. KAHN, JR. "Ooff!! (Sob!) Eep!! (Gulp!) Zowie!!!" *The New Yorker* (November 29 and December 6, 1947). Essentially biographical, two-part profile, but does have something to say about the tremendous popularity of Capp and his strip and the way "Li'l Abner" has developed. Probably the most useful discussion of Capp that has appeared in the popular press.

"The Talk of the Town," *The New Yorker* (October 26, 1963). Interview with Capp, an important source of information on his attitudes in general, and his ideas about the Shmoo in particular.

By Capp

"Charlie Chaplin," *Theatre Arts* (June, 1950). Statement on his theory of comedy, that most men are terribly plagued by feelings of inadequacy and need to be reassured.

Index

SUBJECTS

COMIC STRIPS AND COMIC STRIP CHARACTERS

204

Index

205